Color By Number Adult Coloring Book

This Adult Color By Number Book belongs to:

_____

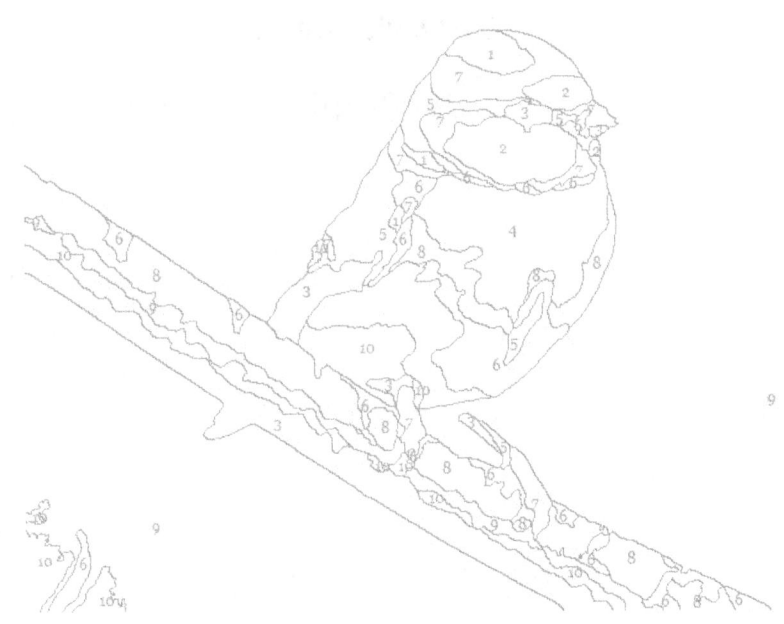

1. Blue

2. Dark Blue

3. Black

4. Yellow

5. Green

6. Brown

7. Dark Blue

8. Gold

9. Dark Green

10. Purple

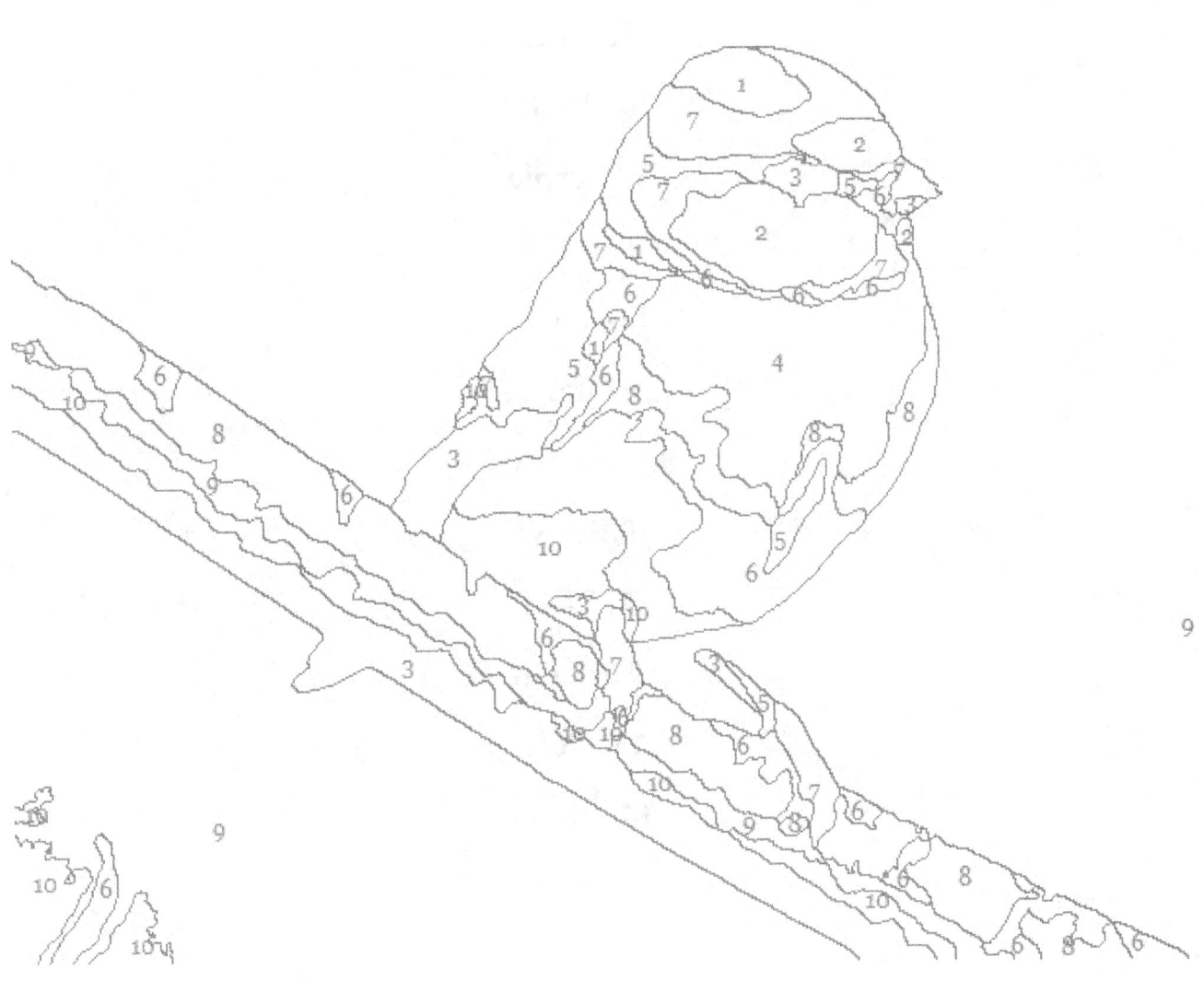

1. Red

2. Green

3. Blue

4. Pink

5. Purple

6. Light Blue

7. Light Green

8. Orange

9. Dark Red

10. Brown

11. Black

12. Dark Green

13. Gold

14. Violet

15. Yellow

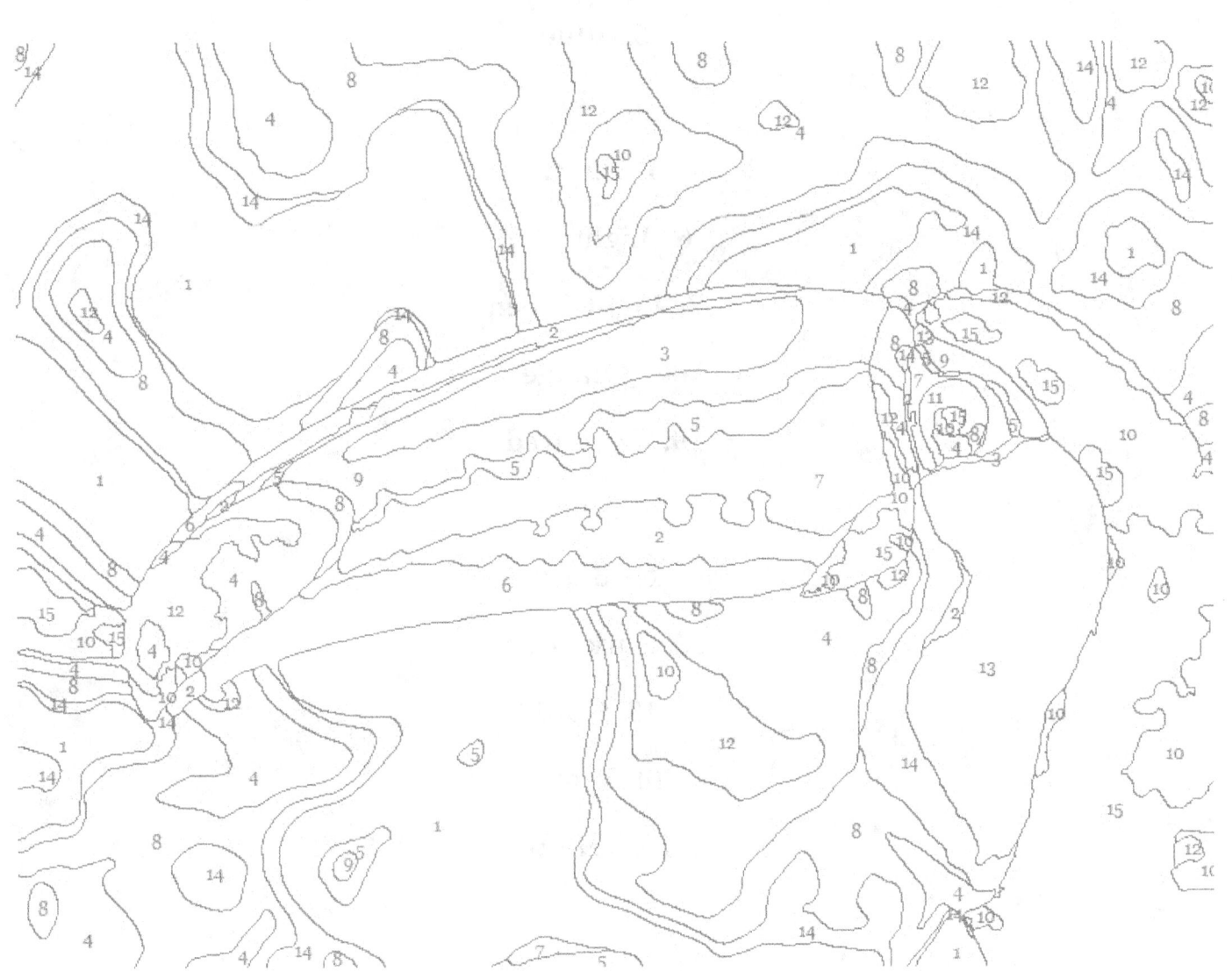

1. Red

2. Green

3. Blue

4. Pink

5. Purple

6. Light Blue

7. Light Green

8. Orange

9. Dark Red

10. Brown

11. Black

12. Dark Green

13. Gold

14. Violet

15. Yellow

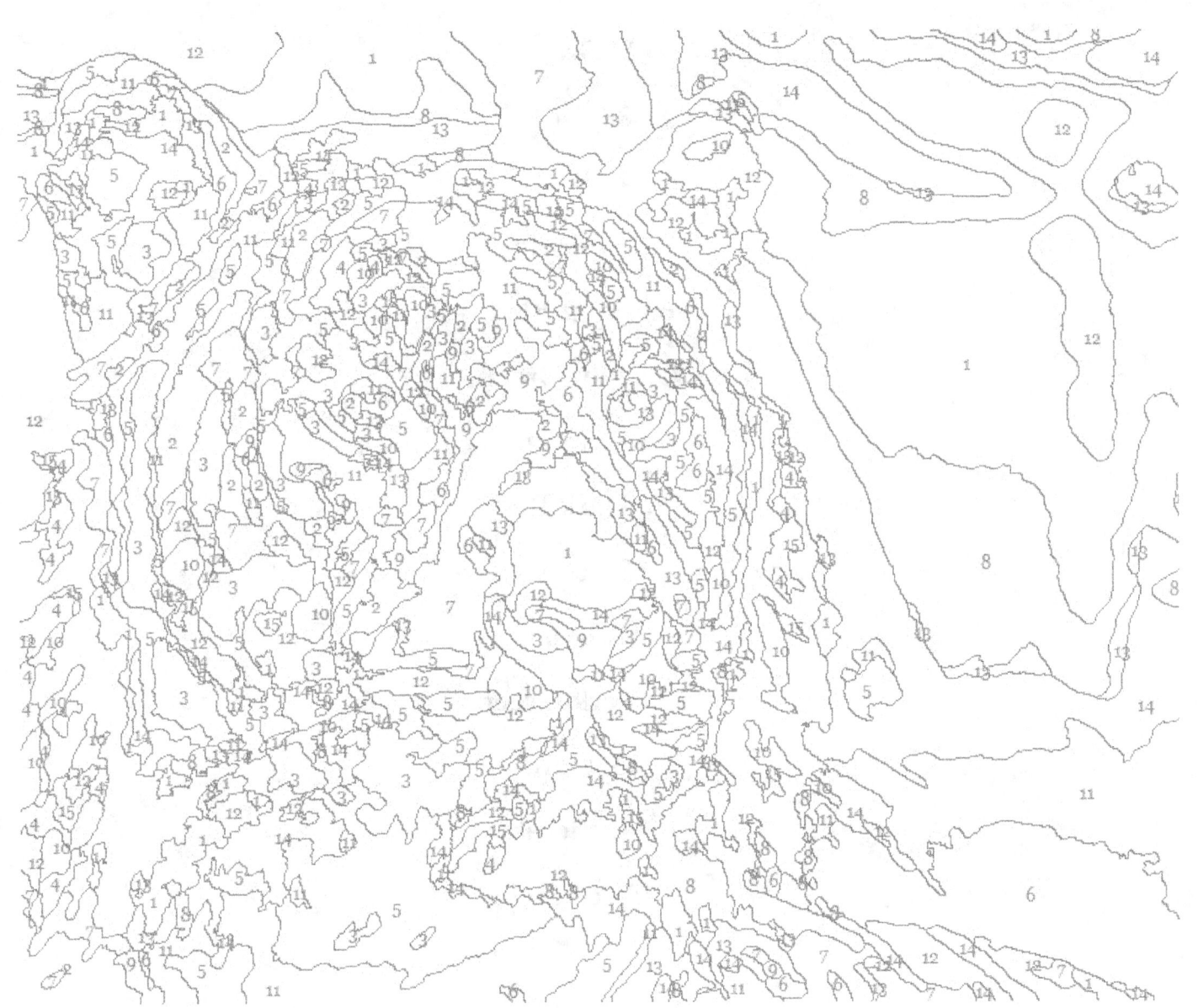

1. Red

2. Green

3. Blue

4. Pink

5. Purple

6. Light Blue

7. Light Green

8. Orange

9. Dark Red

10. Brown

11. Black

12. Dark Green

13. Gold

14. Violet

15. Yellow

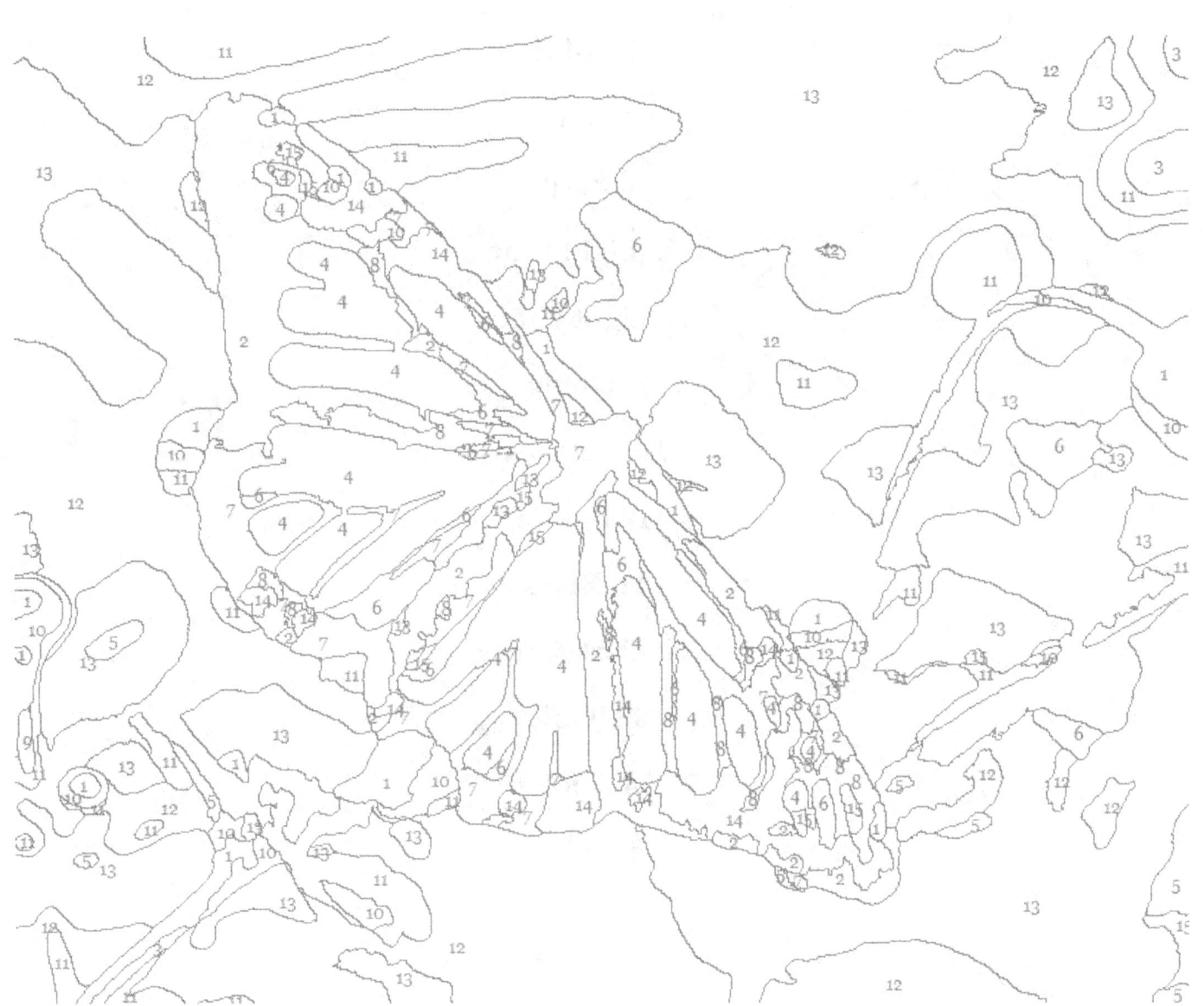

1. Red

2. Green

3. Blue

4. Pink

5. Purple

6. Light Blue

7. Light Green

8. Orange

9. Dark Red

10.Brown

11. Black

12. Dark Green

13. Gold

14. Violet

15. Yellow

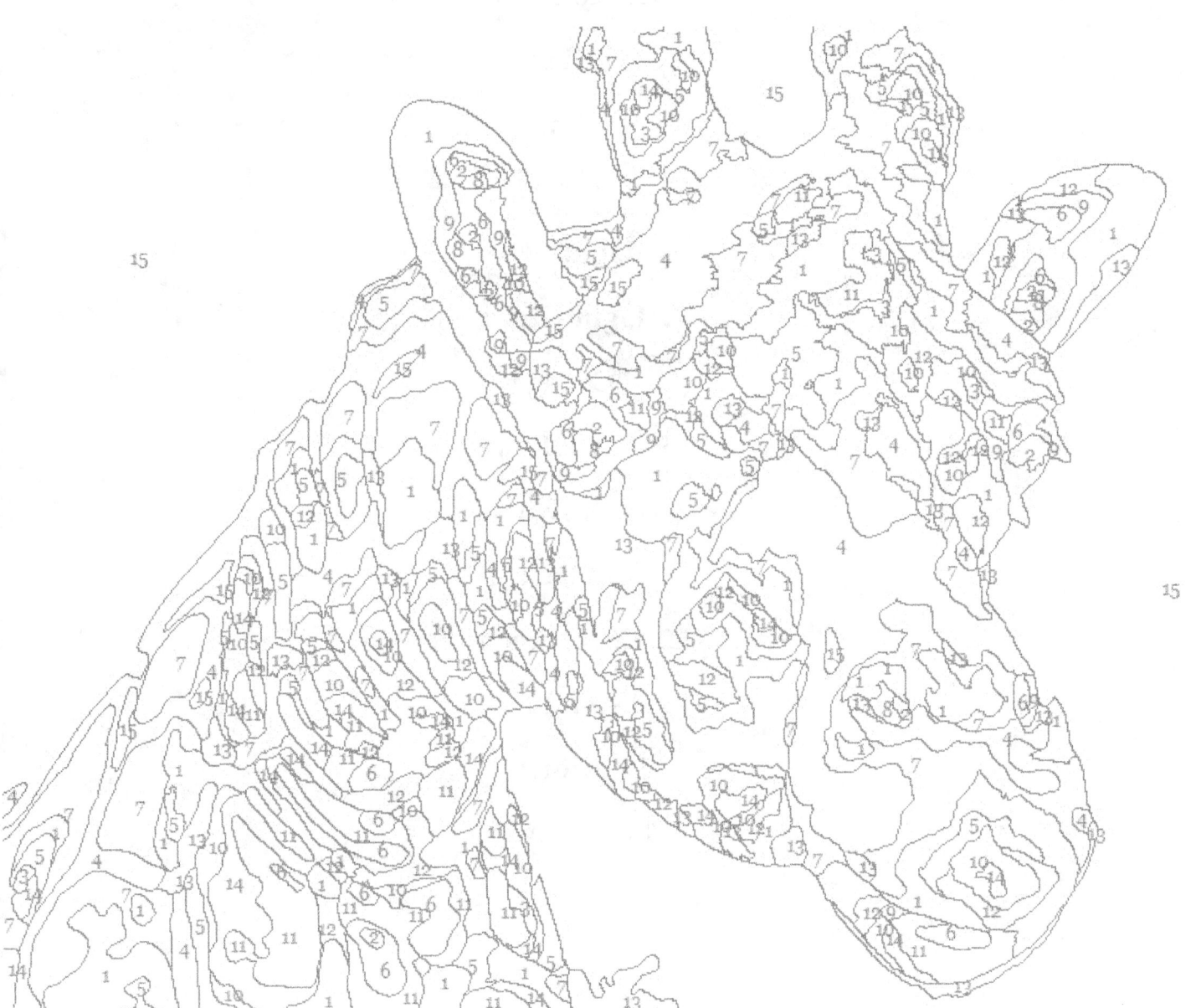

1. Red

2. Green

3. Blue

4. Pink

5. Purple

6. Light Blue

7. Light Green

8. Orange

9. Dark Red

10. Brown

11. Black

12. Dark Green

13. Gold

14. Violet

15. Yellow

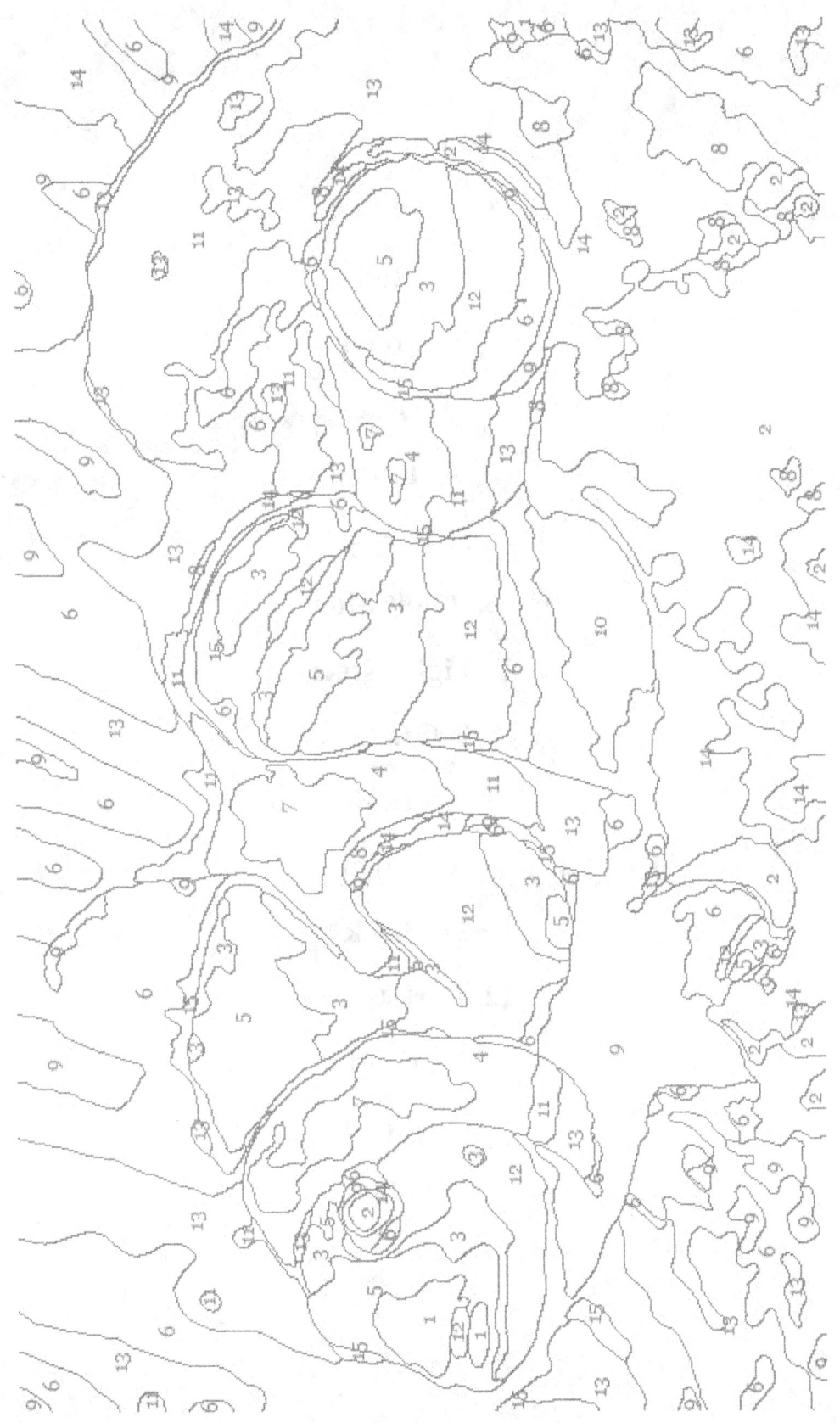

1. Red

2. Green

3. Blue

4. Pink

5. Purple

6. Light Blue

7. Light Green

8. Orange

9. Dark Red

10. Brown

11. Black

12. Dark Green

13. Gold

14. Violet

15. Yellow

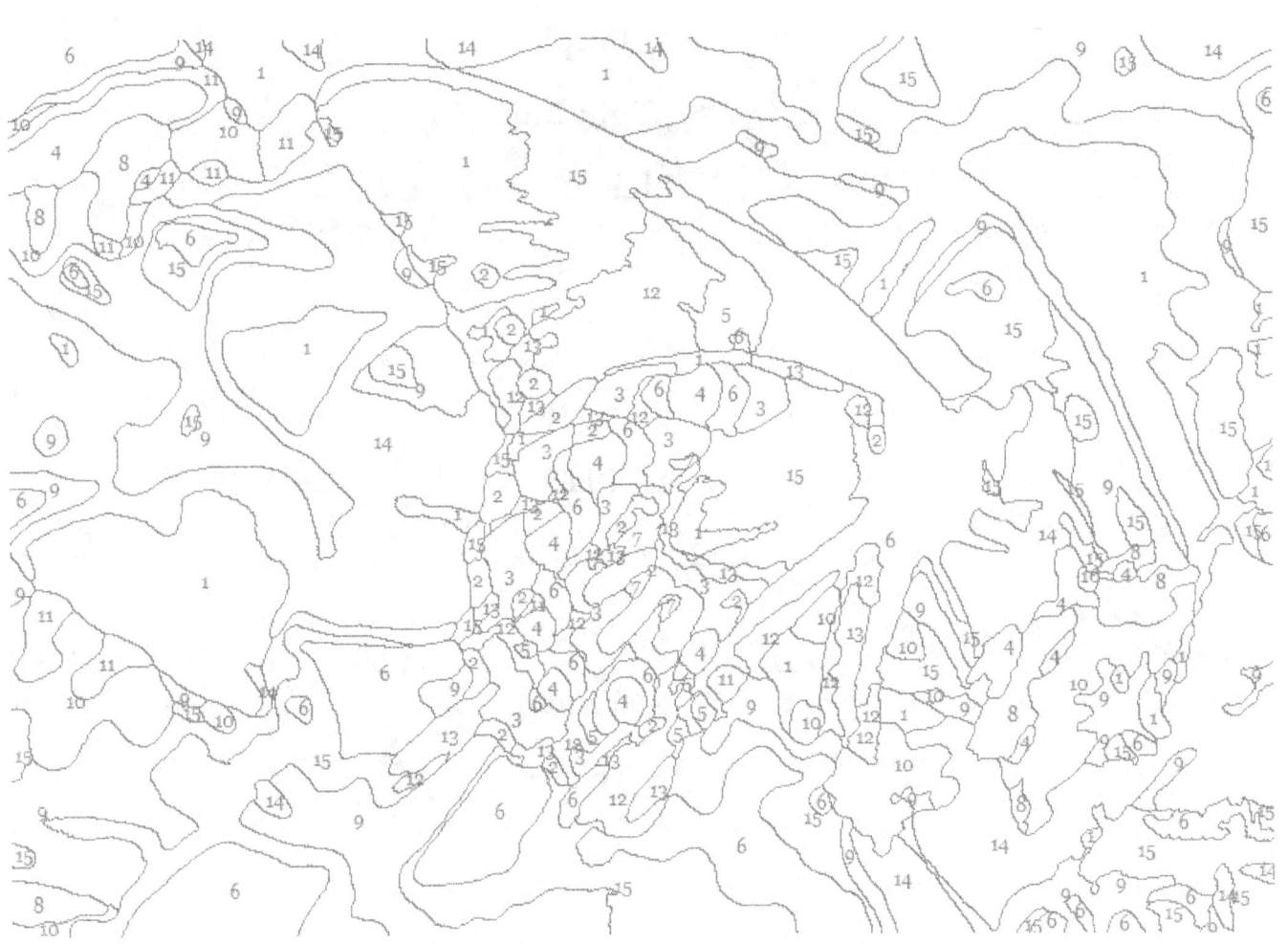

1. Red

2. Green

3. Blue

4. Pink

5. Purple

6. Light Blue

7. Light Green

8. Orange

9. Dark Red

10. Brown

11. Black

12. Dark Green

13. Gold

14. Violet

15. Yellow

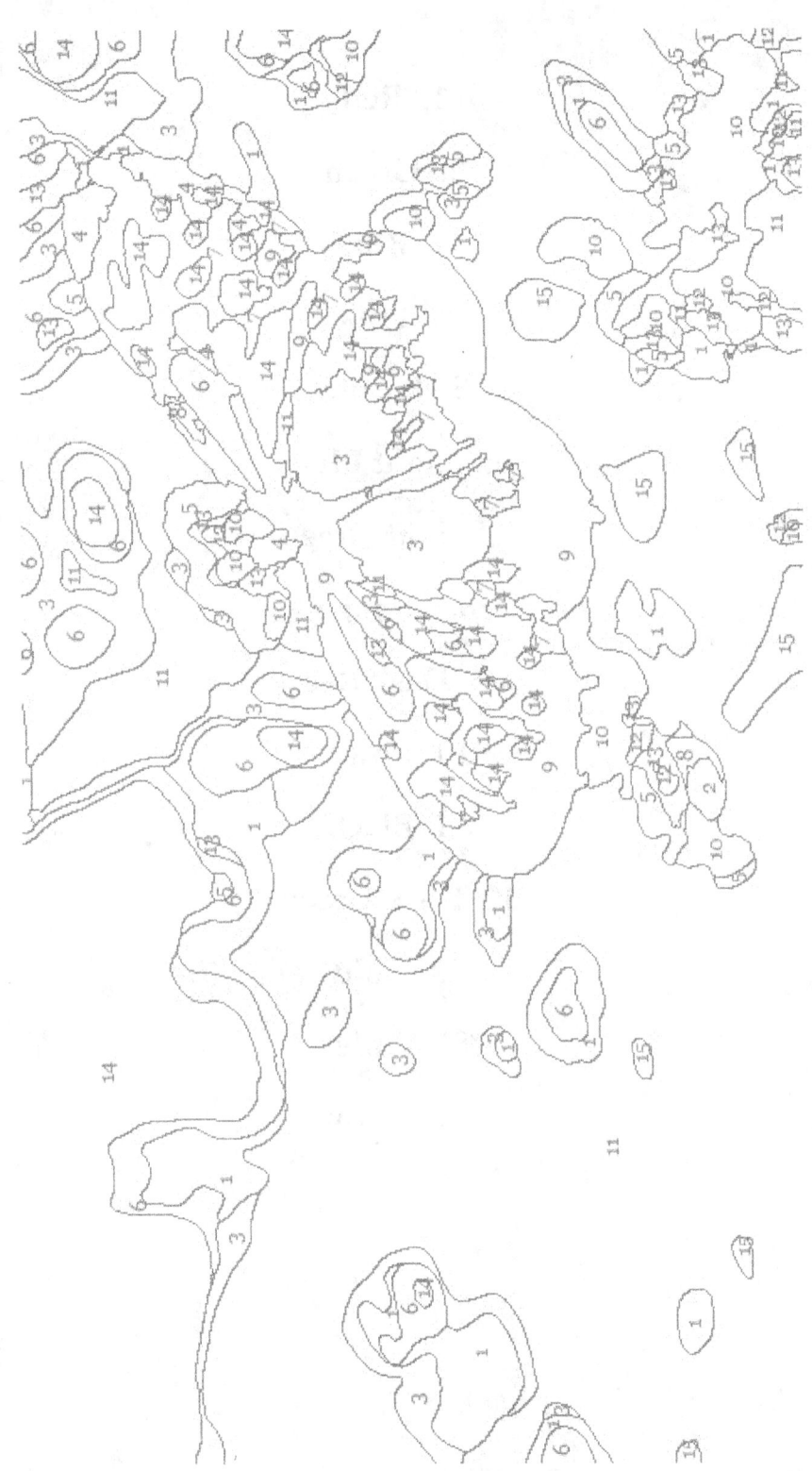

1. Red

2. Green

3. Blue

4. Pink

5. Purple

6. Light Blue

7. Light Green

8. Orange

9. Dark Red

10. Brown

11. Black

12. Dark Green

13. Gold

14. Violet

15. Yellow

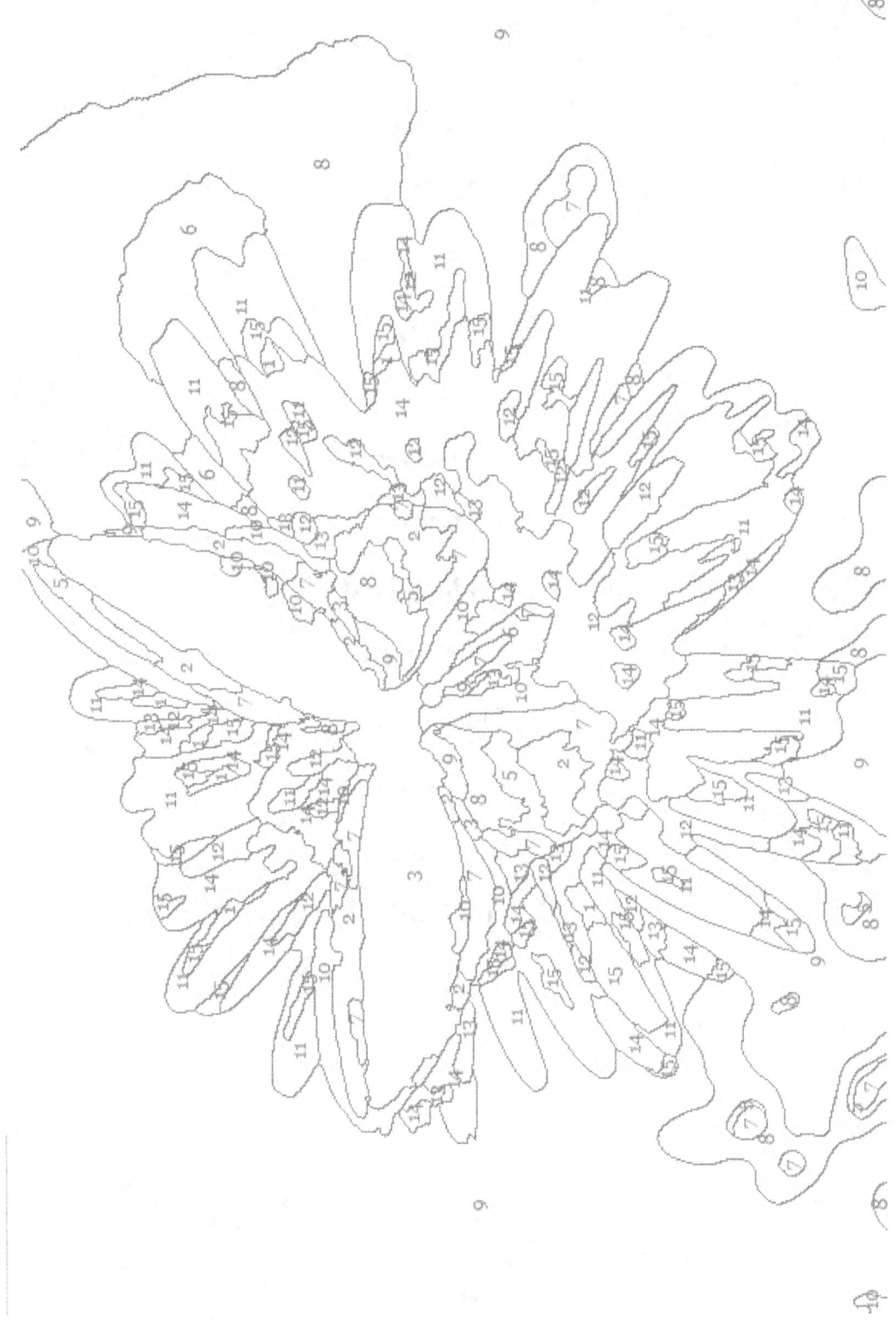

1. Red

2. Green

3. Blue

4. Pink

5. Purple

6. Light Blue

7. Light Green

8. Orange

9. Dark Red

10. Brown

11. Black

12. Dark Green

13. Gold

14. Violet

15. Yellow

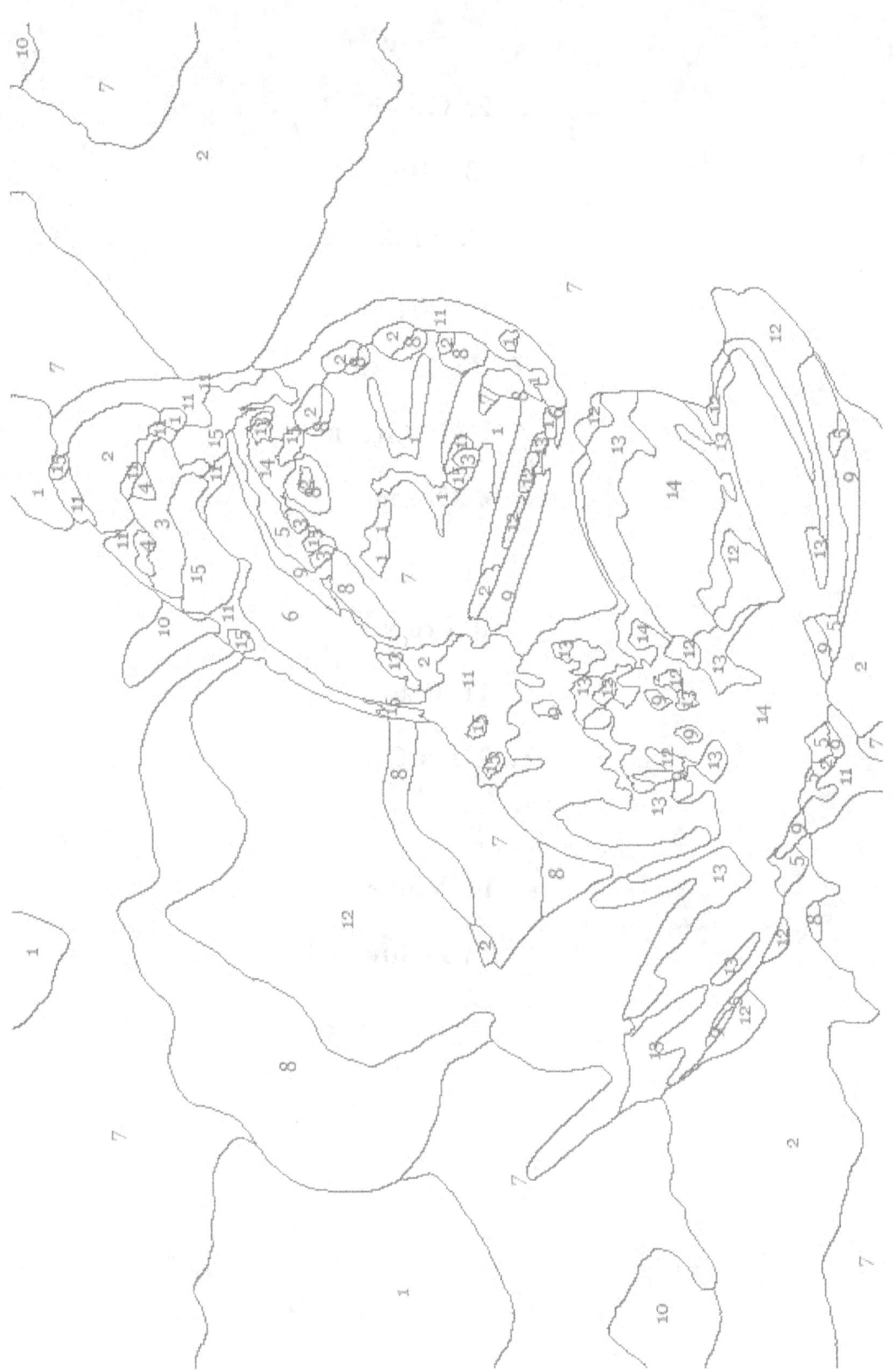

1. Red

2. Green

3. Blue

4. Pink

5. Purple

6. Light Blue

7. Light Green

8. Orange

9. Dark Red

10. Brown

11. Black

12. Dark Green

13. Gold

14. Violet

15. Yellow

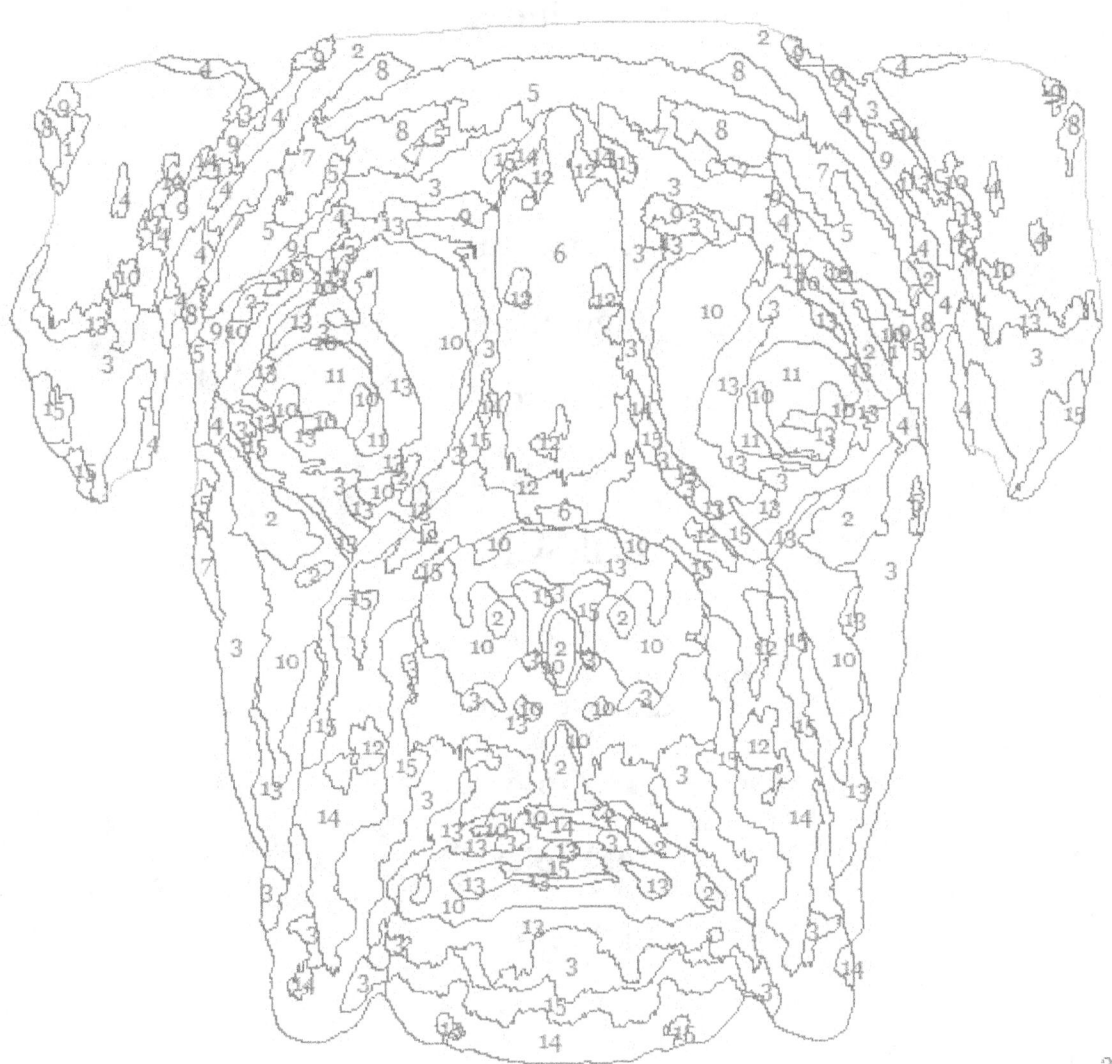

2

1. Red

2. Green

3. Blue

4. Pink

5. Purple

6. Light Blue

7. Light Green

8. Orange

9. Dark Red

10. Brown

11. Black

12. Dark Green

13. Gold

14. Violet

15. Yellow

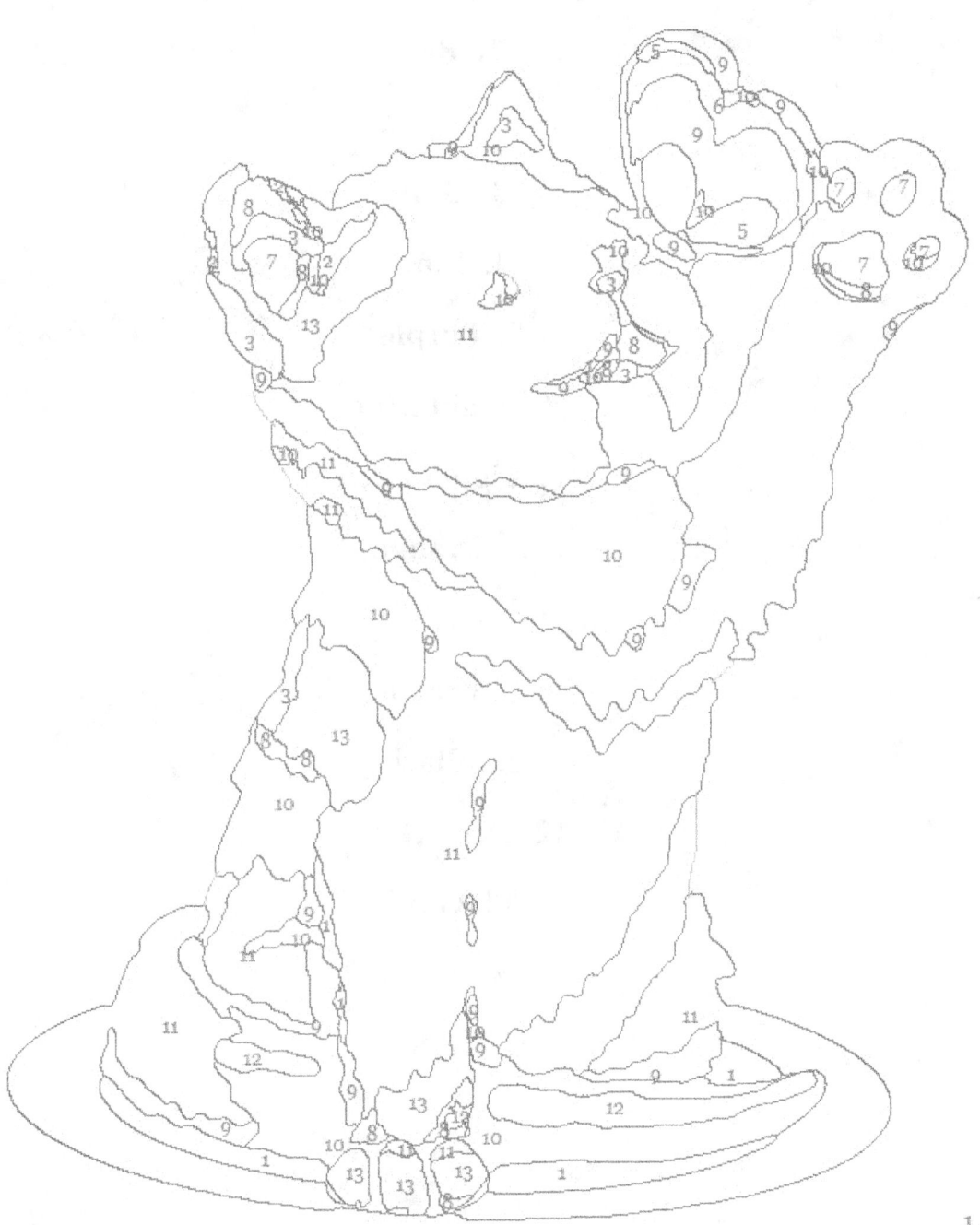

1. Red

2. Green

3. Blue

4. Pink

5. Purple

6. Light Blue

7. Light Green

8. Orange

9. Dark Red

10. Brown

11. Black

12. Dark Green

13. Gold

14. Violet

15. Yellow

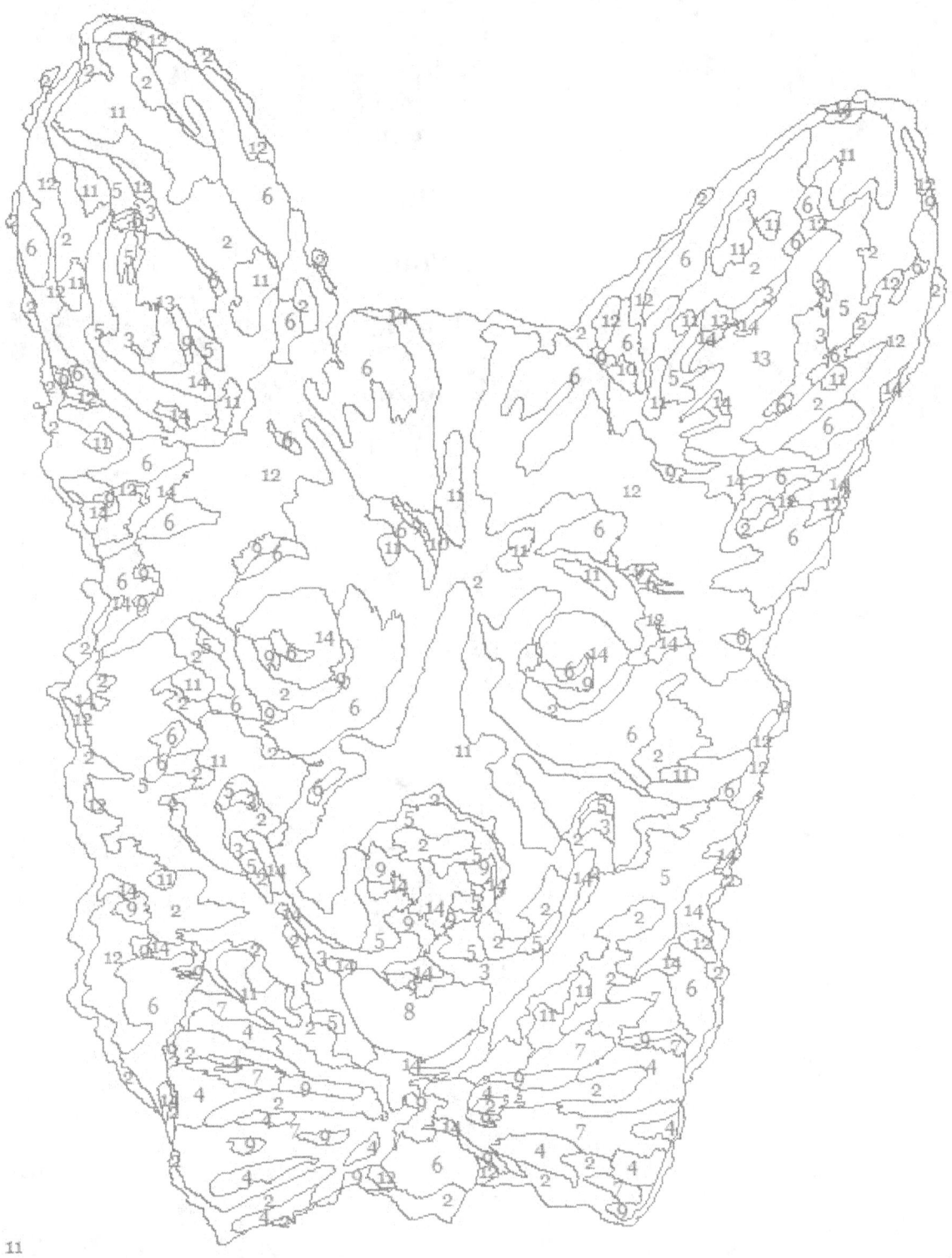

1. Red

2. Green

3. Blue

4. Pink

5. Purple

6. Light Blue

7. Light Green

8. Orange

9. Dark Red

10. Brown

11. Black

12. Dark Green

13. Gold

14. Violet

15. Yellow

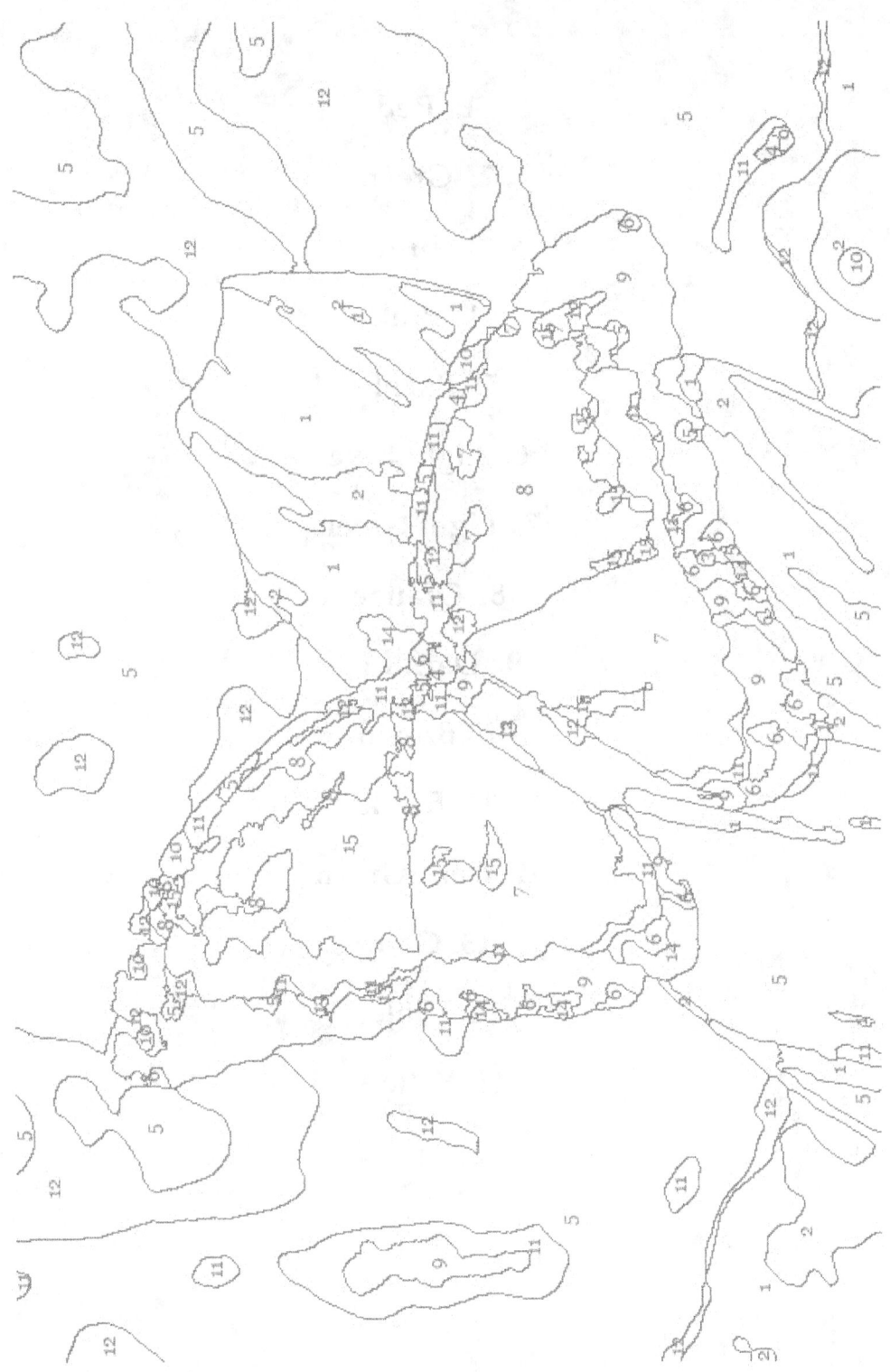

1. Red

2. Green

3. Blue

4. Pink

5. Purple

6. Light Blue

7. Light Green

8. Orange

9. Dark Red

10. Brown

11. Black

12. Dark Green

13. Gold

14. Violet

15. Yellow

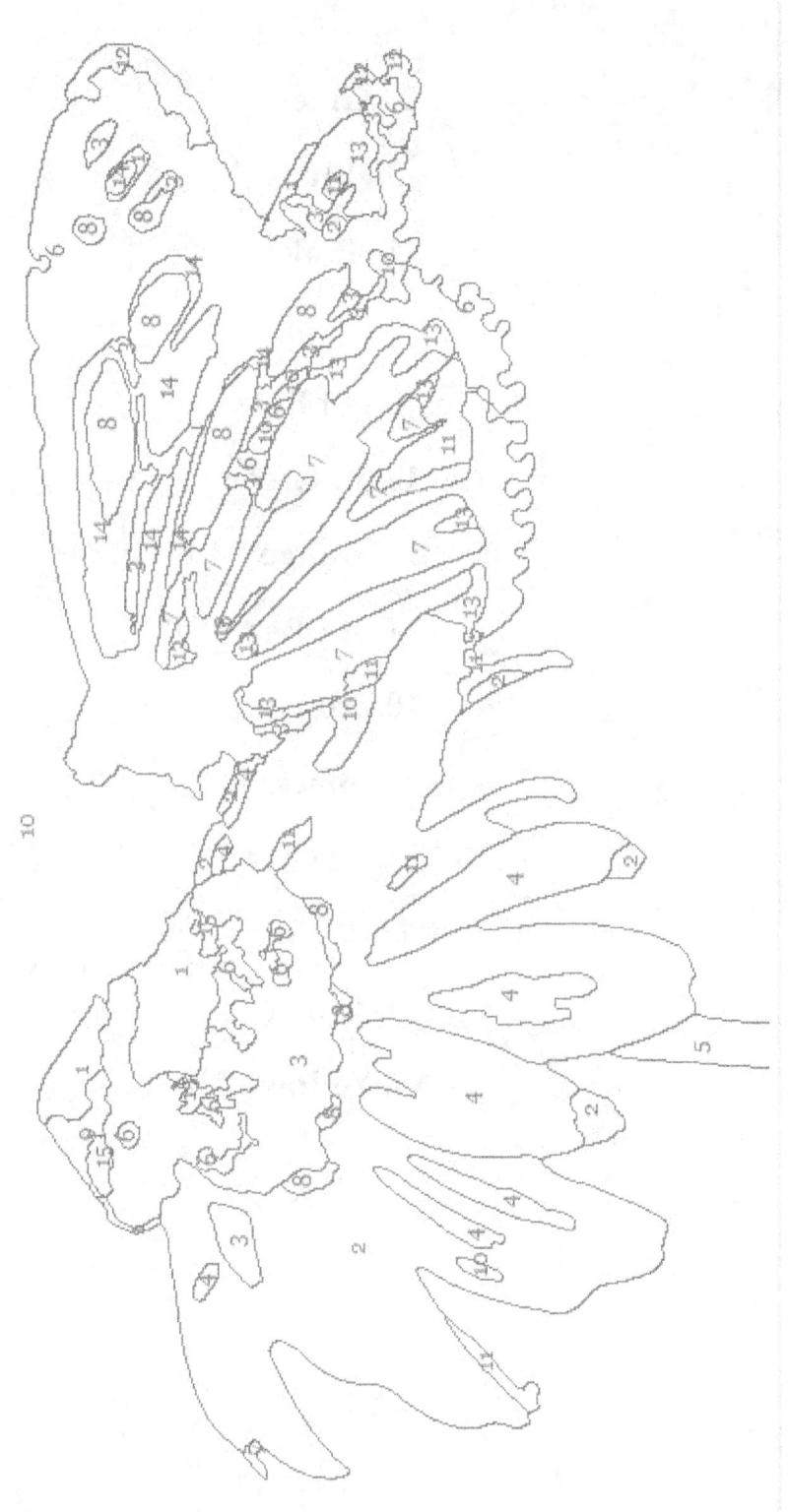

1. Red

2. Green

3. Blue

4. Pink

5. Purple

6. Light Blue

7. Light Green

8. Orange

9. Dark Red

10. Brown

11. Black

12. Dark Green

13. Gold

14. Violet

15. Yellow

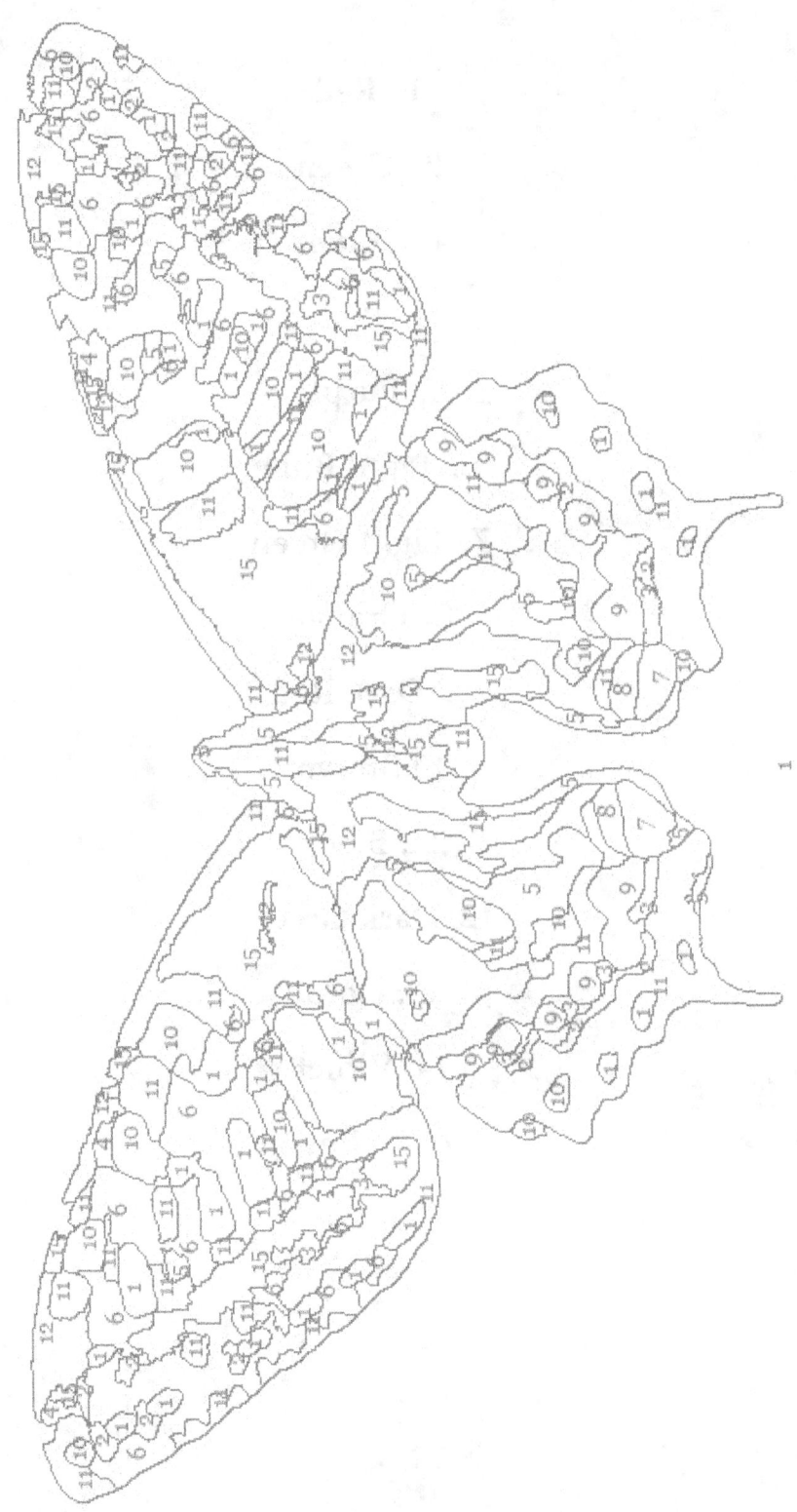

1. Red

2. Green

3. Blue

4. Pink

5. Purple

6. Light Blue

7. Light Green

8. Orange

9. Dark Red

10. Brown

11. Black

12. Dark Green

13. Gold

14. Violet

15. Yellow

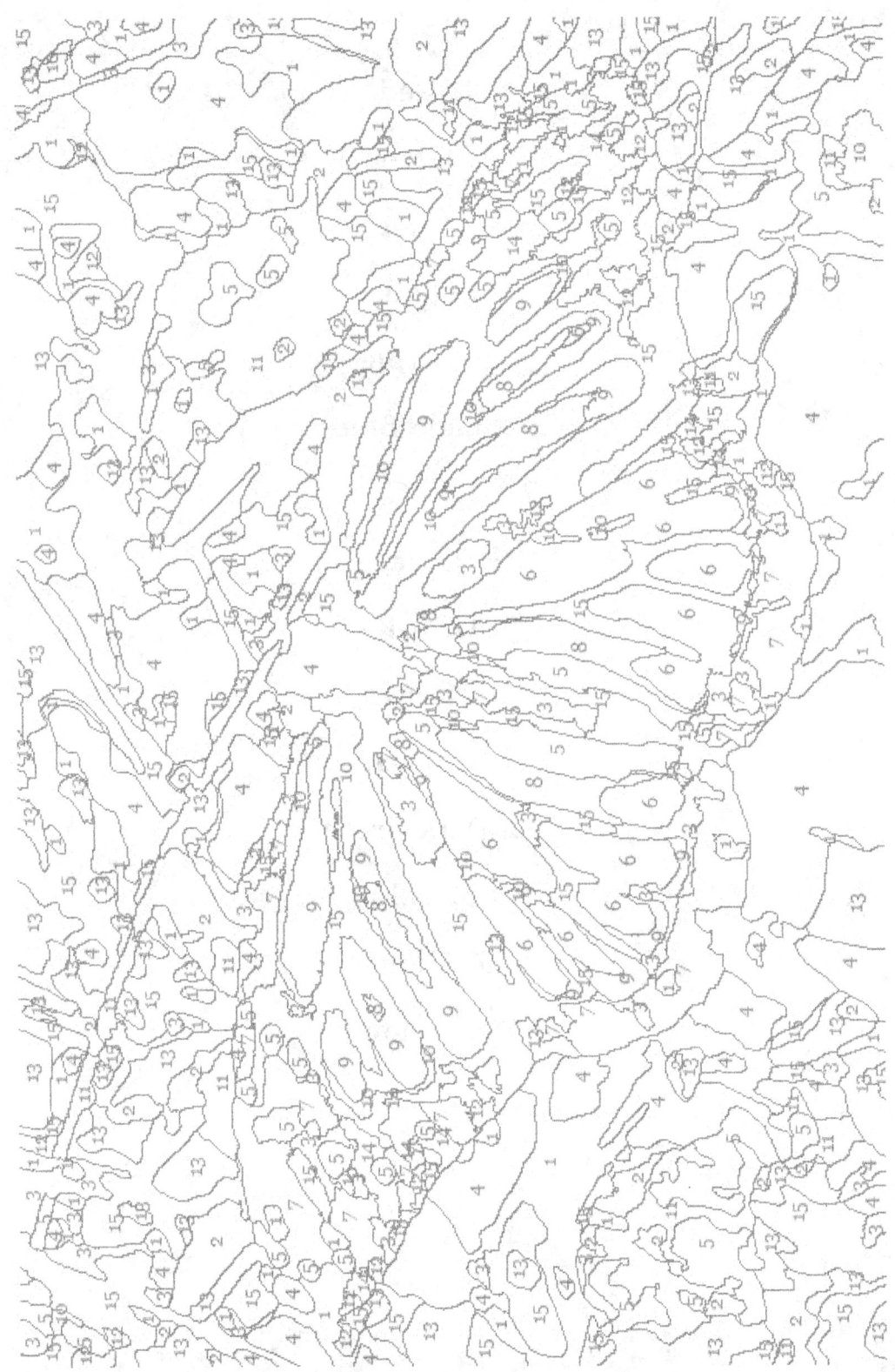

1. Red

2. Green

3. Blue

4. Pink

5. Purple

6. Light Blue

7. Light Green

8. Orange

9. Dark Red

10. Brown

11. Black

12. Dark Green

13. Gold

14. Violet

15. Yellow

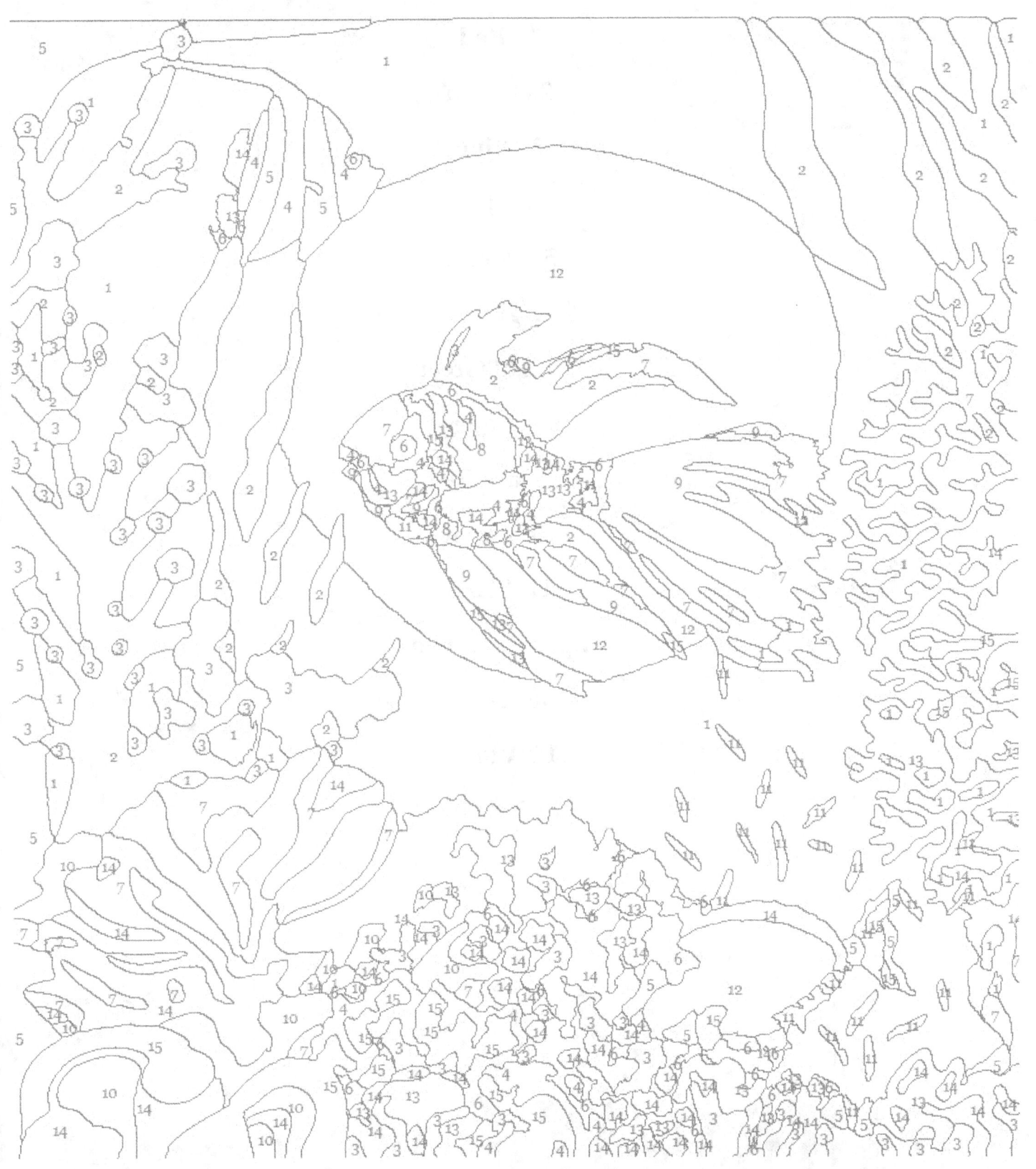

1. Red

2. Green

3. Blue

4. Pink

5. Purple

6. Light Blue

7. Light Green

8. Orange

9. Dark Red

10. Brown

11. Black

12. Dark Green

13. Gold

14. Violet

15. Yellow

7

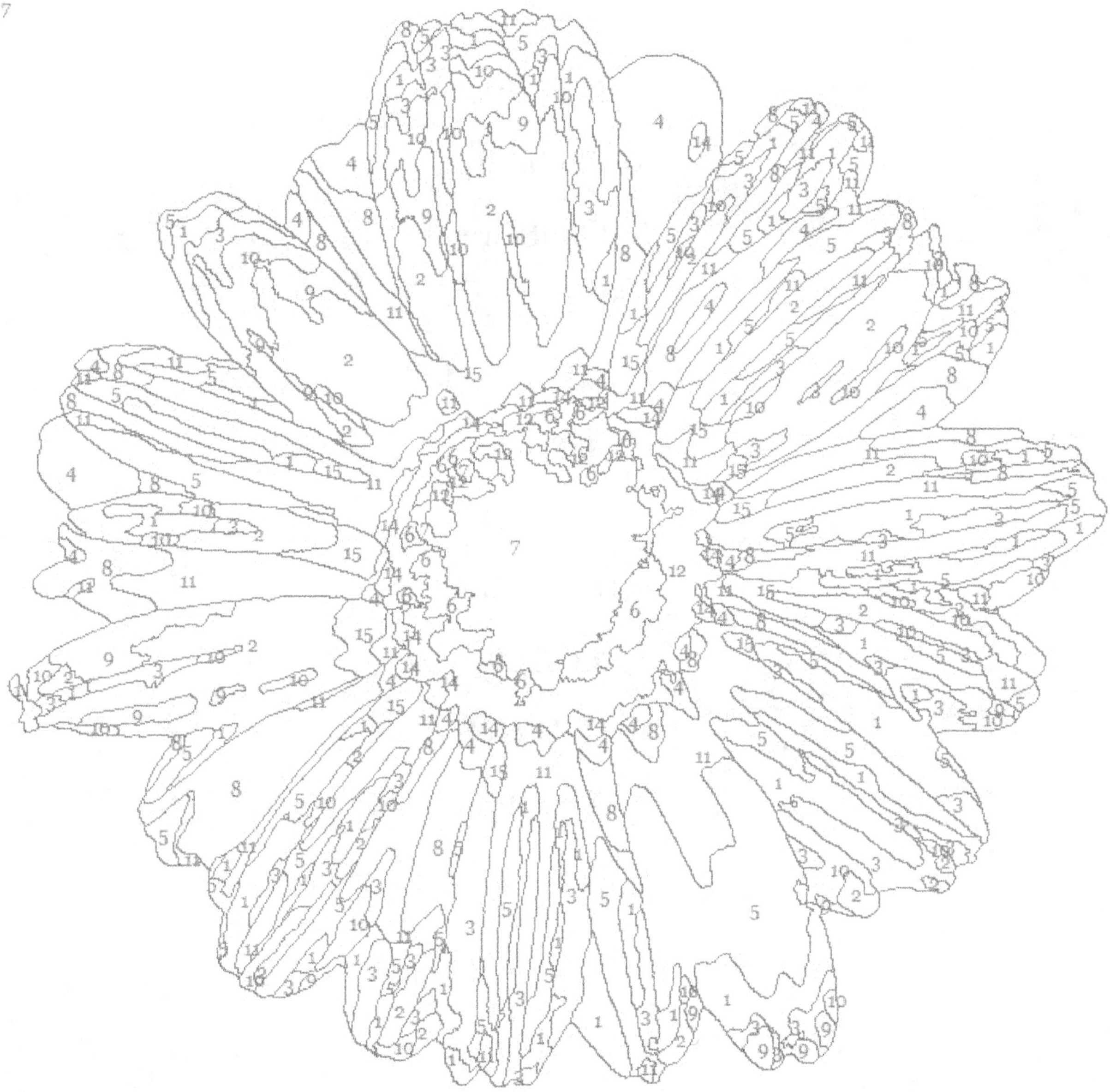

1. Red

2. Green

3. Blue

4. Pink

5. Purple

6. Light Blue

7. Light Green

8. Orange

9. Dark Red

10. Brown

11. Black

12. Dark Green

13. Gold

14. Violet

15. Yellow

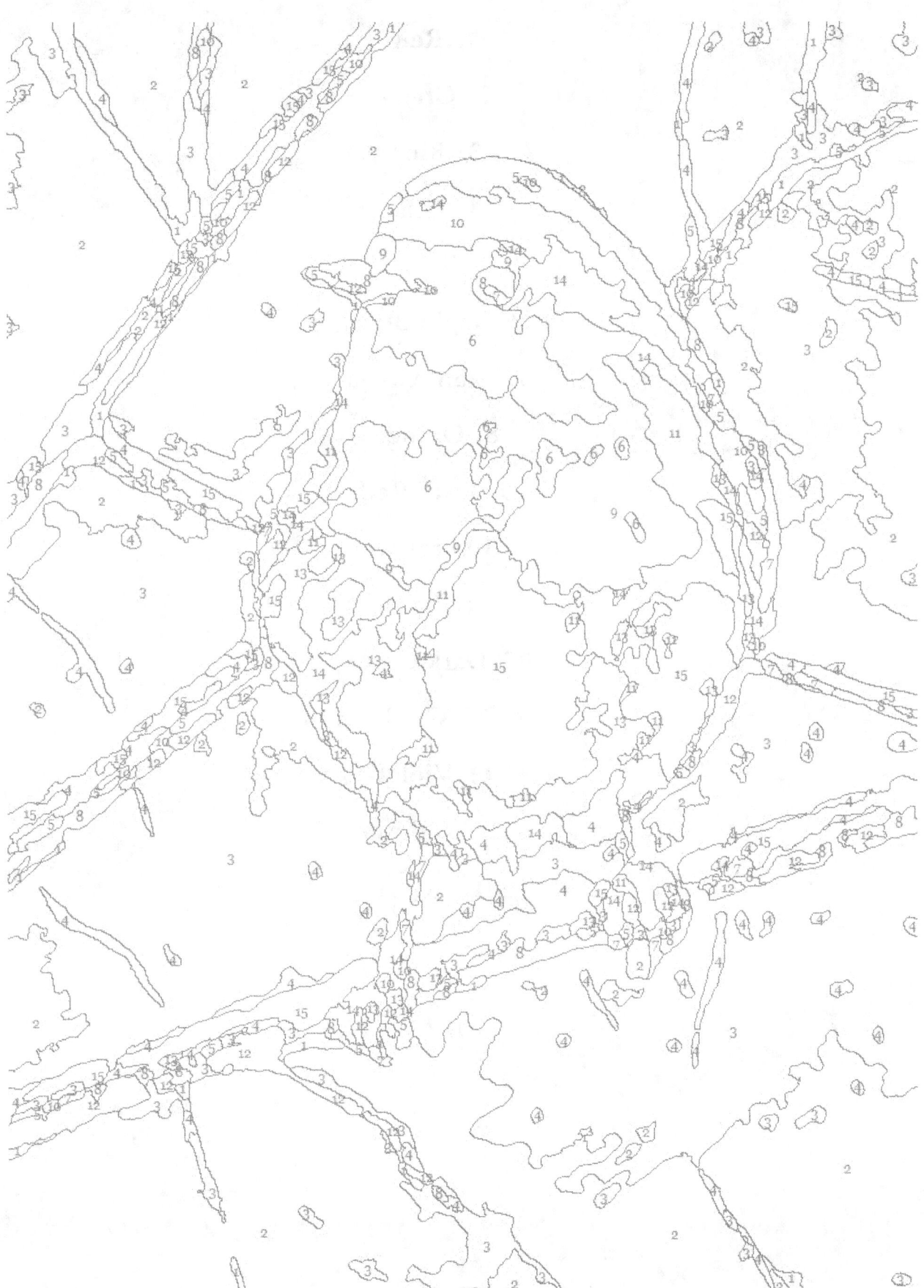

1. Red

2. Green

3. Blue

4. Pink

5. Purple

6. Light Blue

7. Light Green

8. Orange

9. Dark Red

10. Brown

11. Black

12. Dark Green

13. Gold

14. Violet

15. Yellow

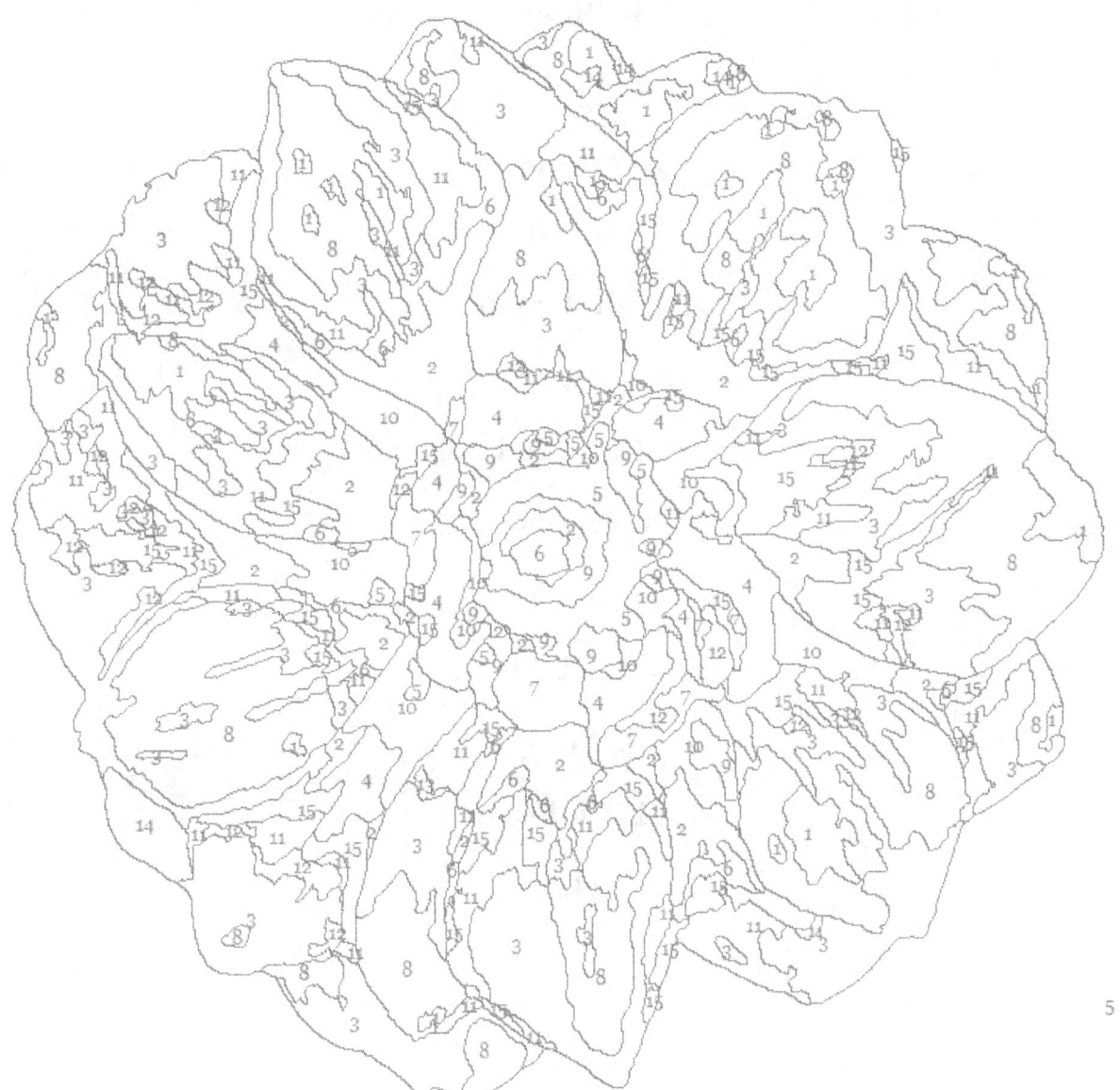

5

1. Red

2. Green

3. Blue

4. Pink

5. Purple

6. Light Blue

7. Light Green

8. Orange

9. Dark Red

10. Brown

11. Black

12. Dark Green

13. Gold

14. Violet

15. Yellow

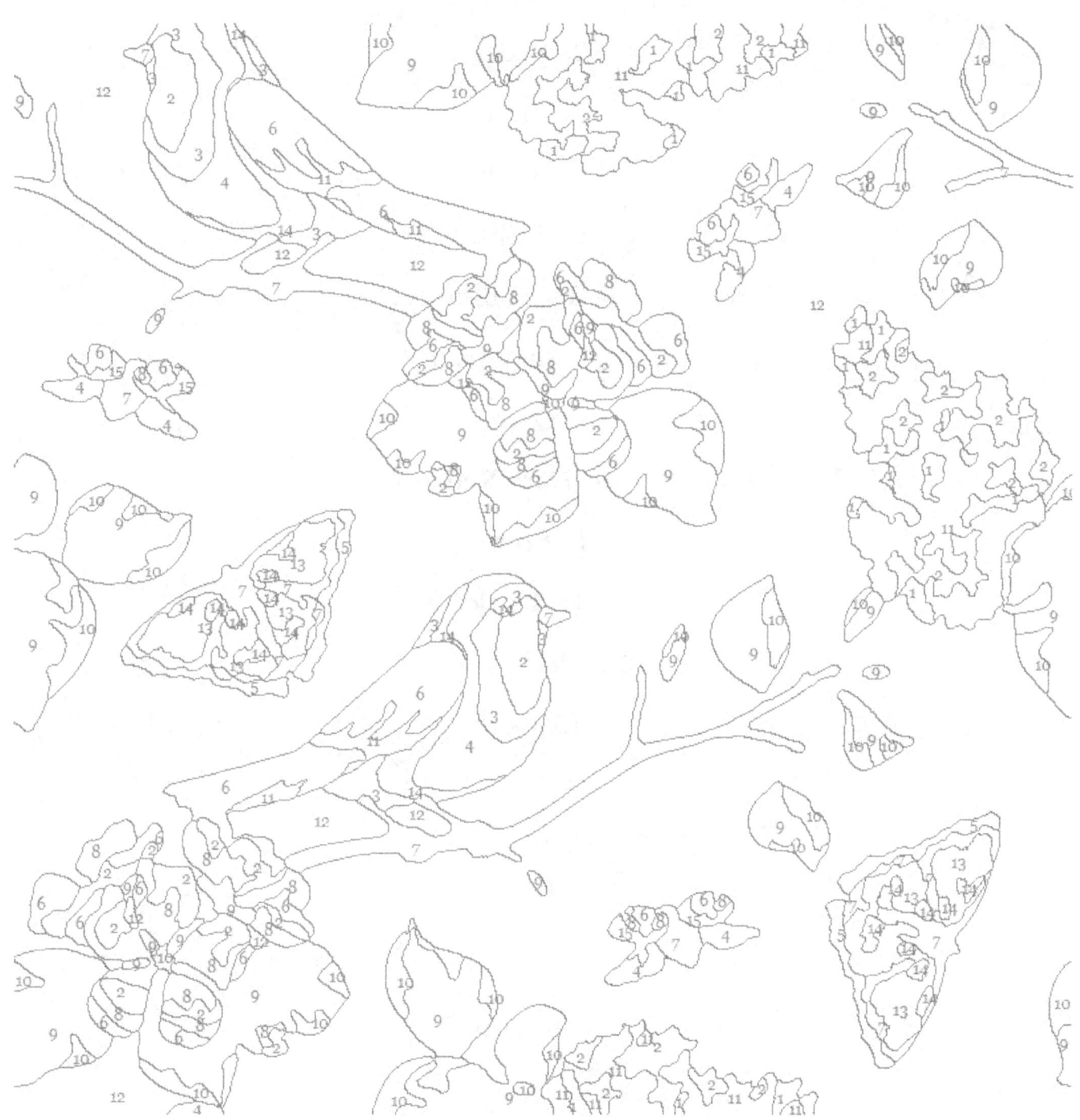

1. Red

2. Green

3. Blue

4. Pink

5. Purple

6. Light Blue

7. Light Green

8. Orange

9. Dark Red

10.Brown

11. Black

12. Dark Green

13. Gold

14. Violet

15. Yellow

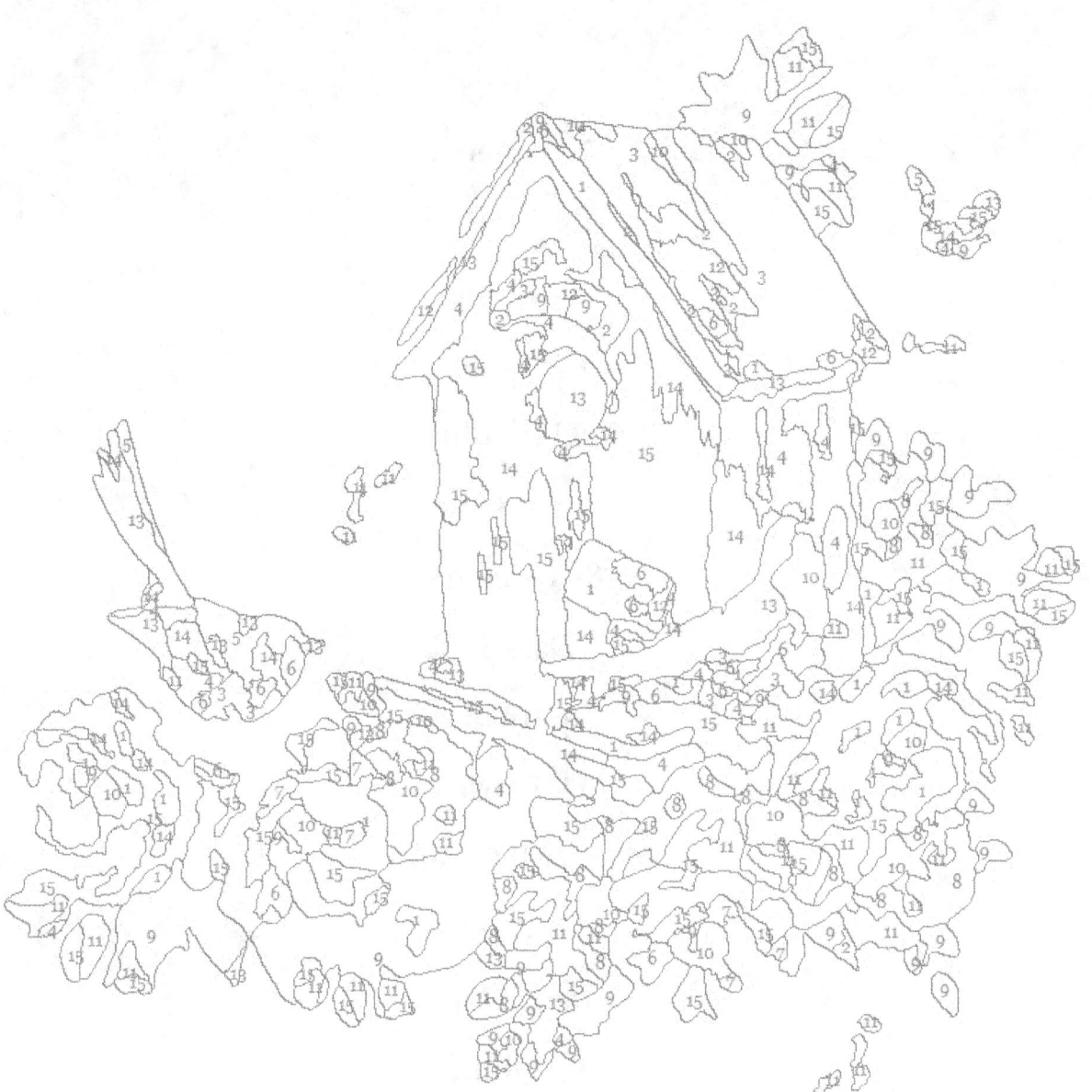

1

1. Red

2. Green

3. Blue

4. Pink

5. Purple

6. Light Blue

7. Light Green

8. Orange

9. Dark Red

10. Brown

11. Black

12. Dark Green

13. Gold

14. Violet

15. Yellow

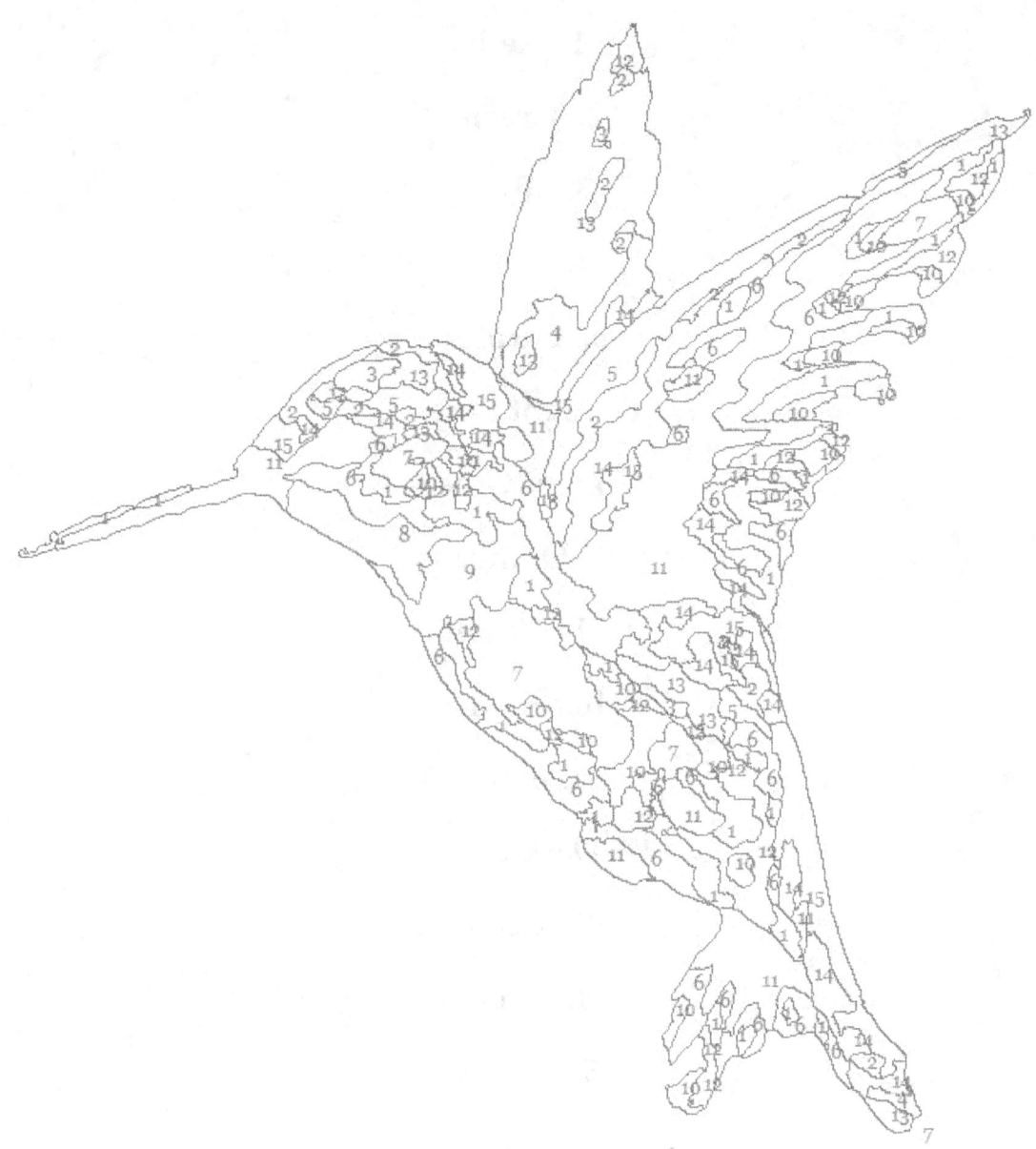

1. Red

2. Green

3. Blue

4. Pink

5. Purple

6. Light Blue

7. Light Green

8. Orange

9. Dark Red

10. Brown

11. Black

12. Dark Green

13. Gold

14. Violet

15. Yellow

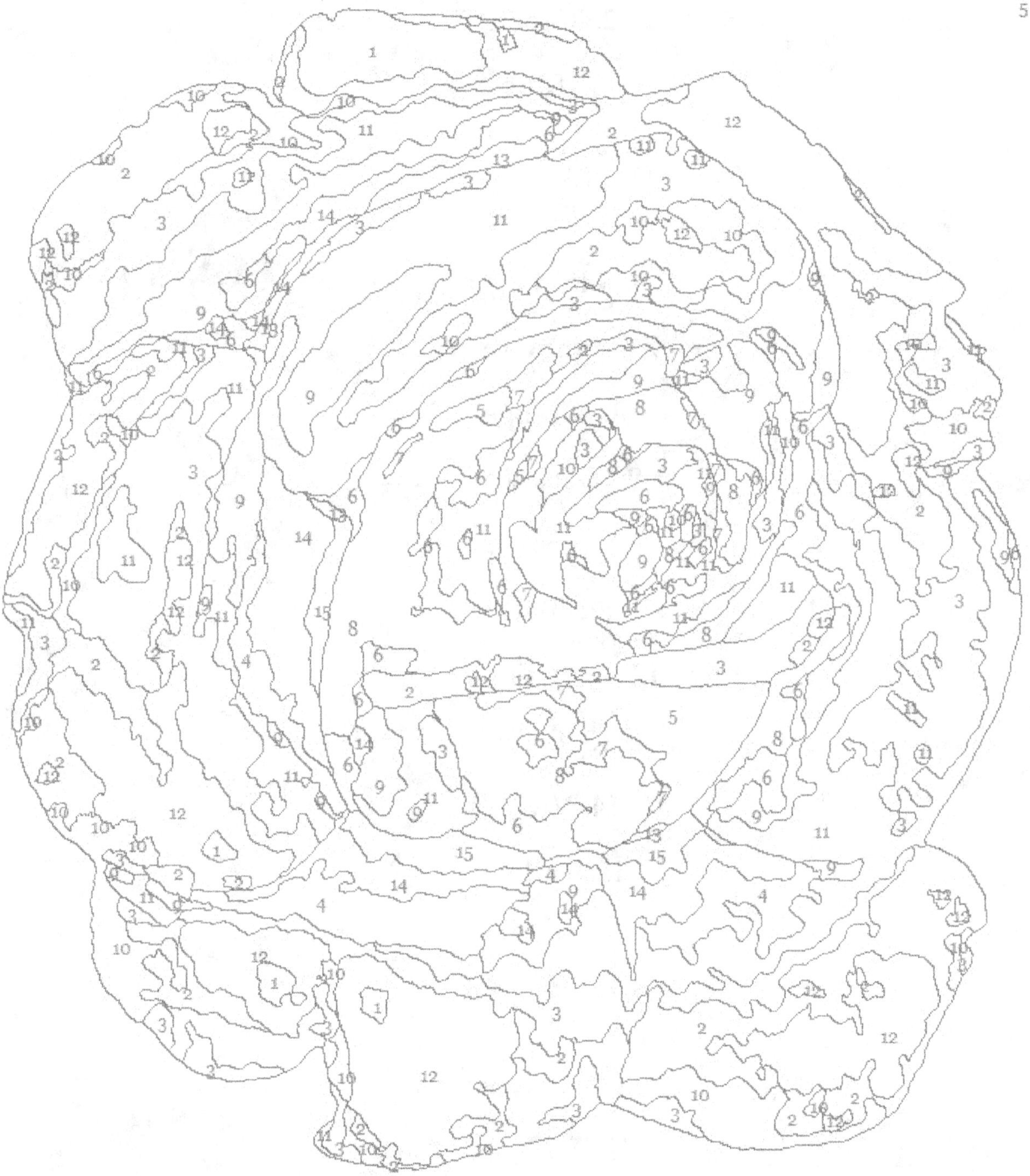

1. Red

2. Green

3. Blue

4. Pink

5. Purple

6. Light Blue

7. Light Green

8. Orange

9. Dark Red

10. Brown

11. Black

12. Dark Green

13. Gold

14. Violet

15. Yellow

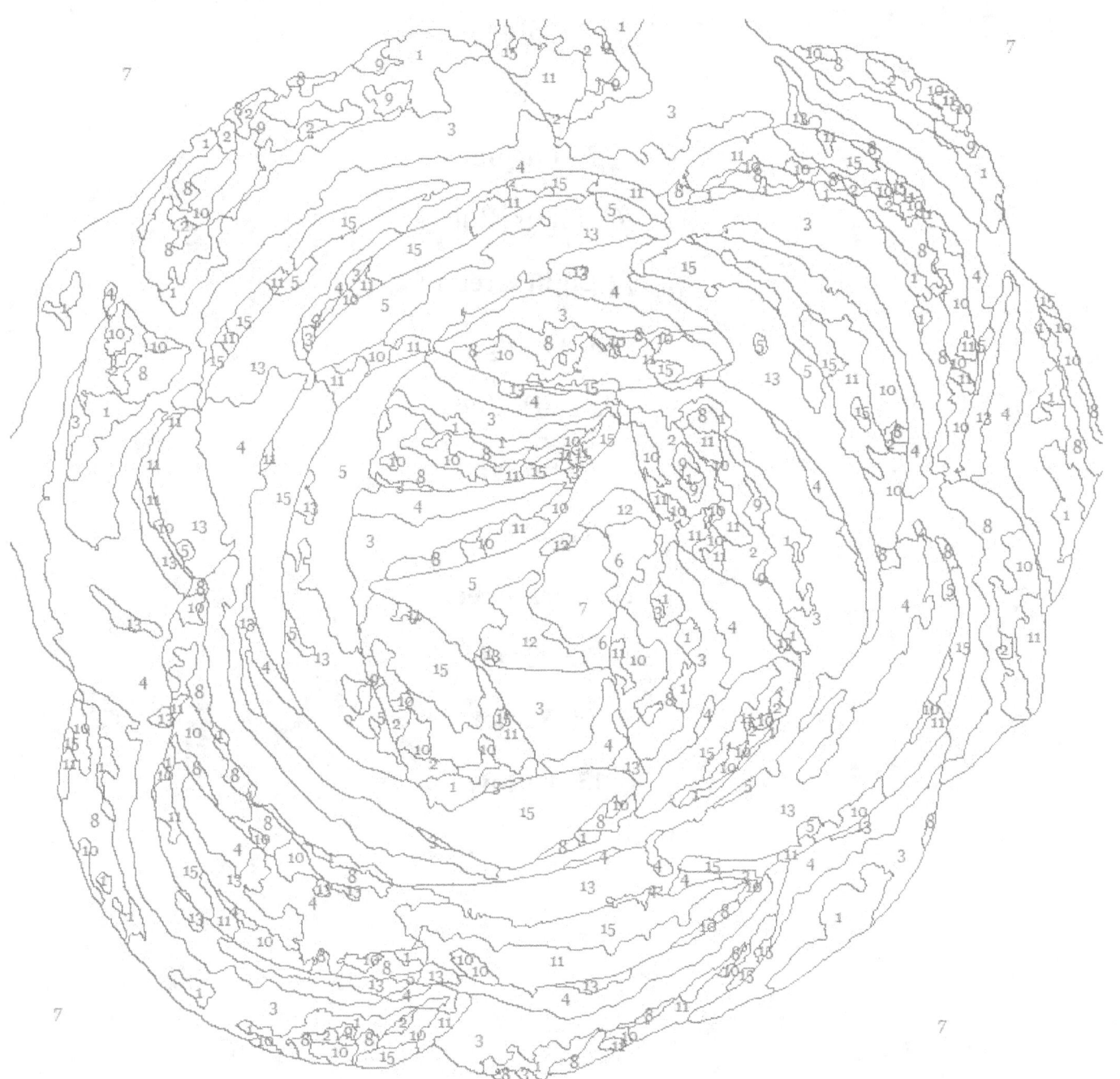

1. Red

2. Green

3. Blue

4. Pink

5. Purple

6. Light Blue

7. Light Green

8. Orange

9. Dark Red

10. Brown

11. Black

12. Dark Green

13. Gold

14. Violet

15. Yellow

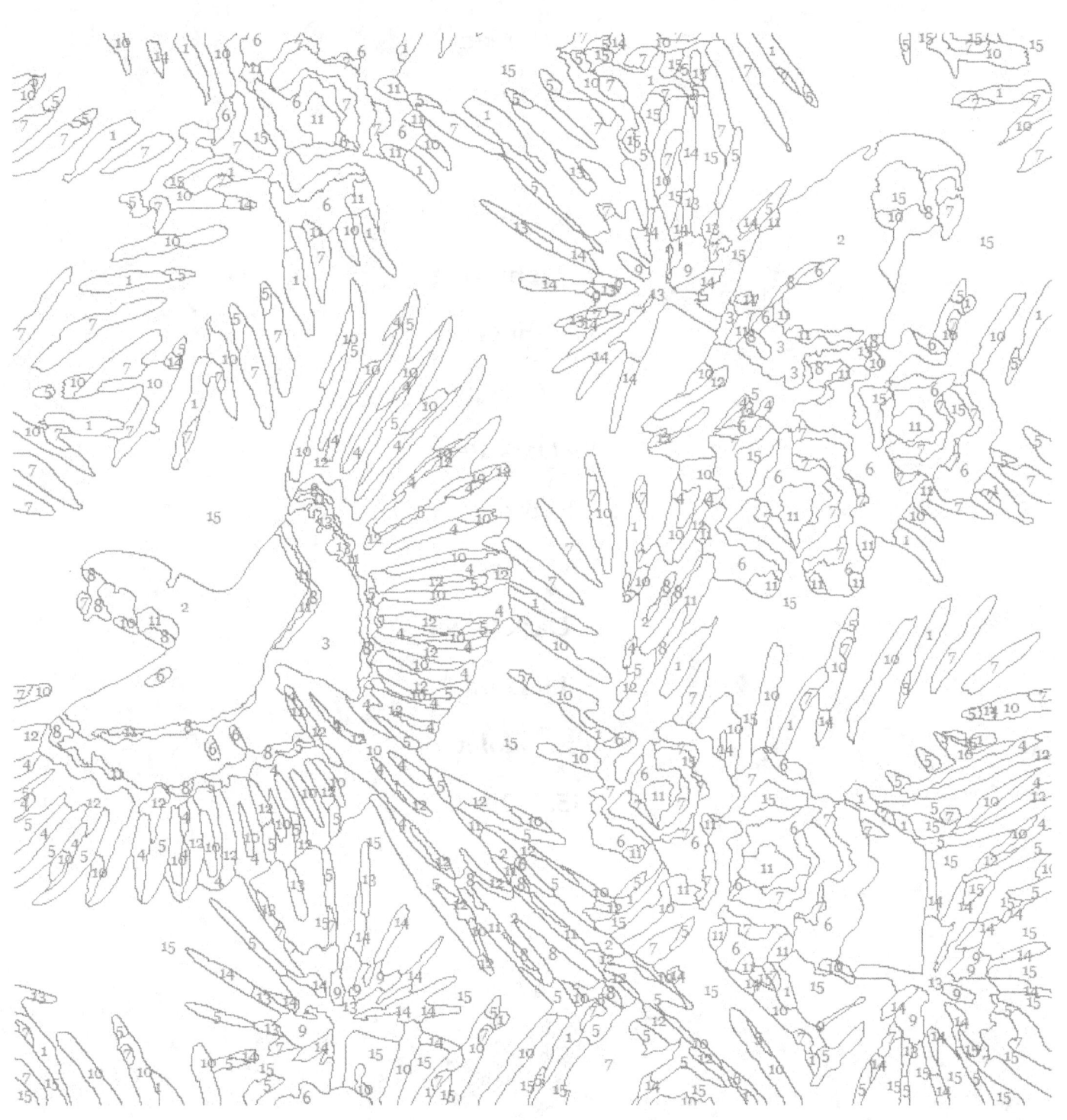

1. Red

2. Green

3. Blue

4. Pink

5. Purple

6. Light Blue

7. Light Green

8. Orange

9. Dark Red

10. Brown

11. Black

12. Dark Green

13. Gold

14. Violet

15. Yellow

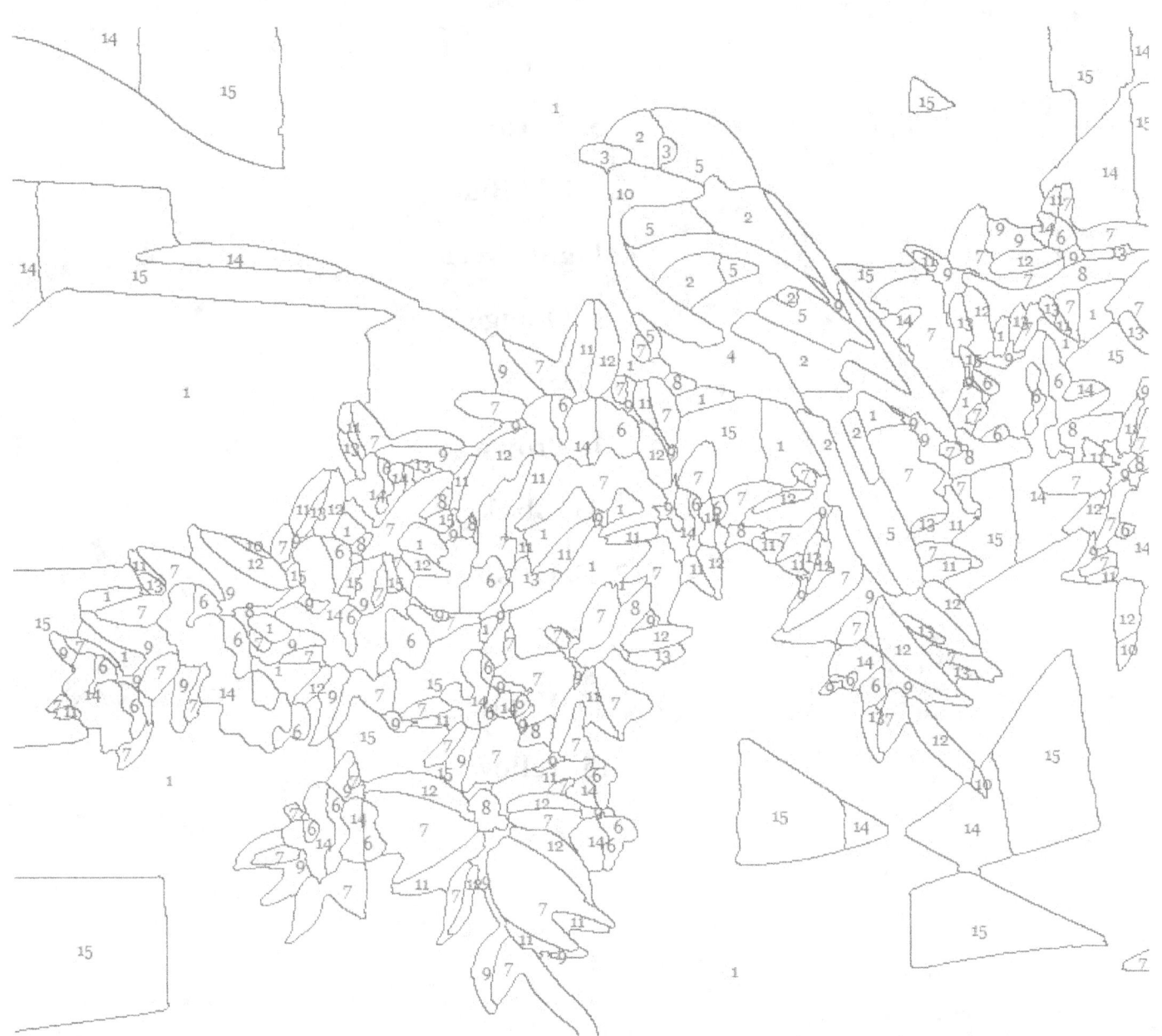

1. Red

2. Green

3. Blue

4. Pink

5. Purple

6. Light Blue

7. Light Green

8. Orange

9. Dark Red

10. Brown

11. Black

12. Dark Green

13. Gold

14. Violet

15. Yellow

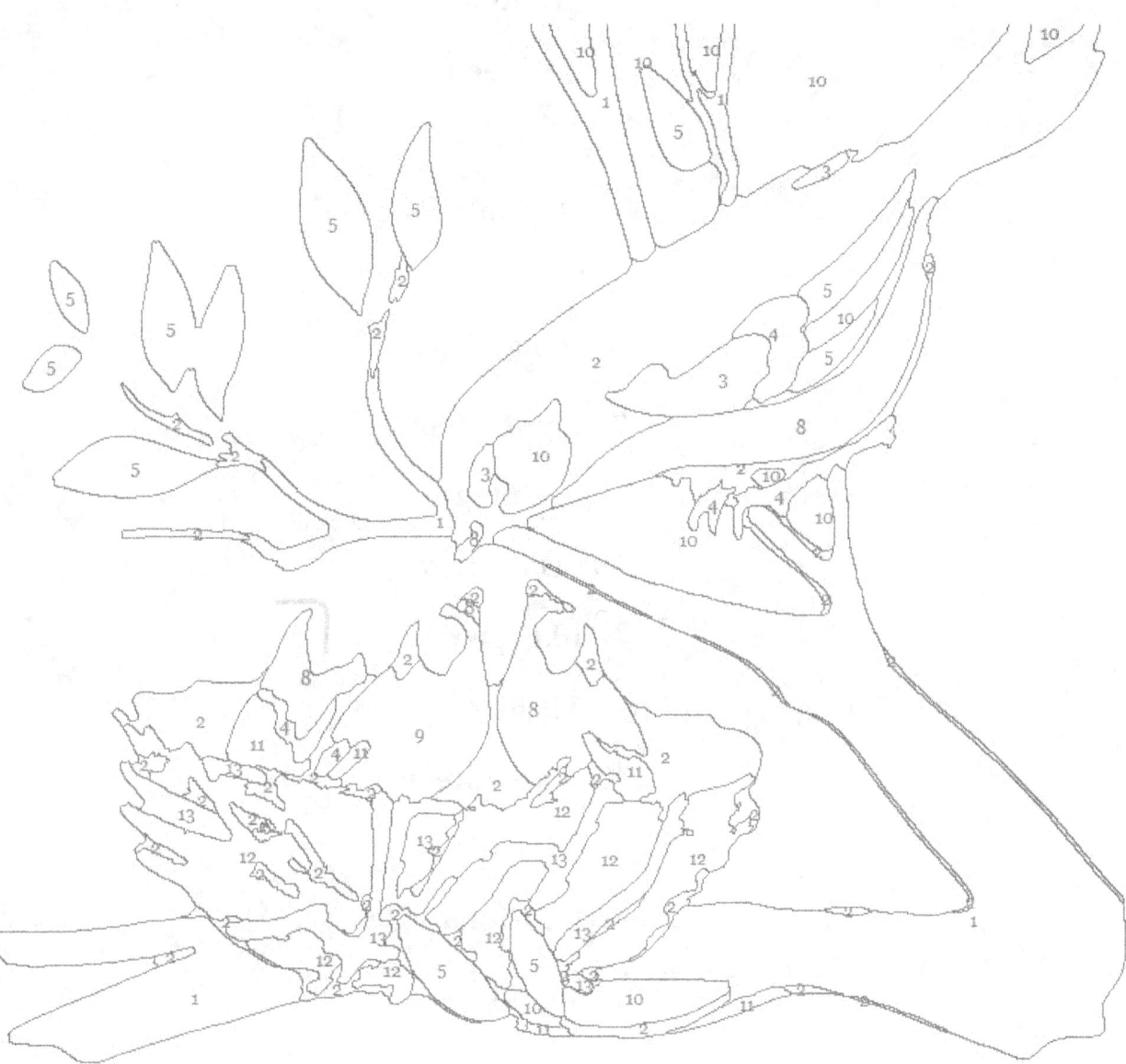

1. Red

2. Green

3. Blue

4. Pink

5. Purple

6. Light Blue

7. Light Green

8. Orange

9. Dark Red

10. Brown

11. Black

12. Dark Green

13. Gold

14. Violet

15. Yellow

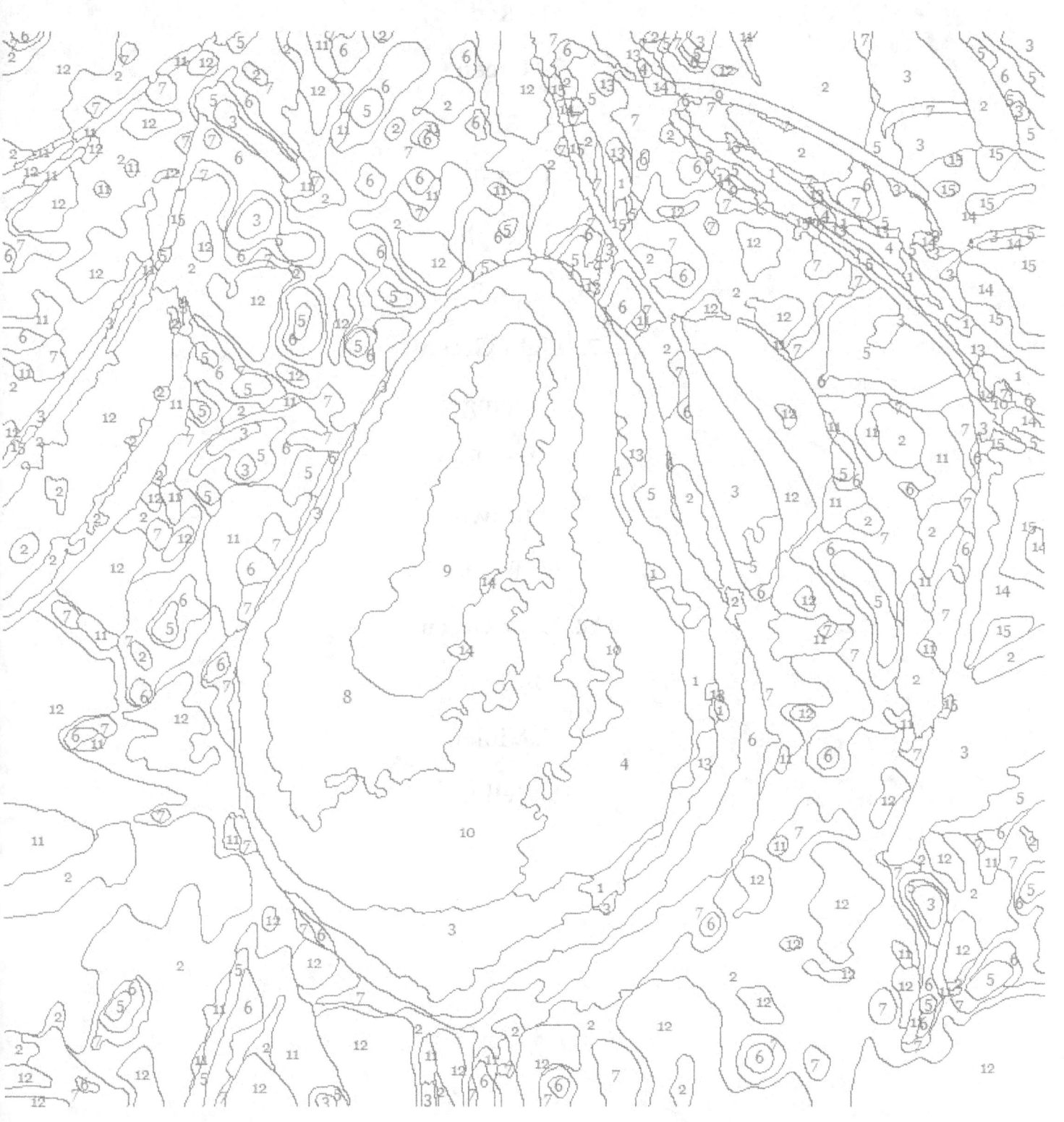

1. Red

2. Green

3. Blue

4. Pink

5. Purple

6. Light Blue

7. Light Green

8. Orange

9. Dark Red

10. Brown

11. Black

12. Dark Green

13. Gold

14. Violet

15. Yellow

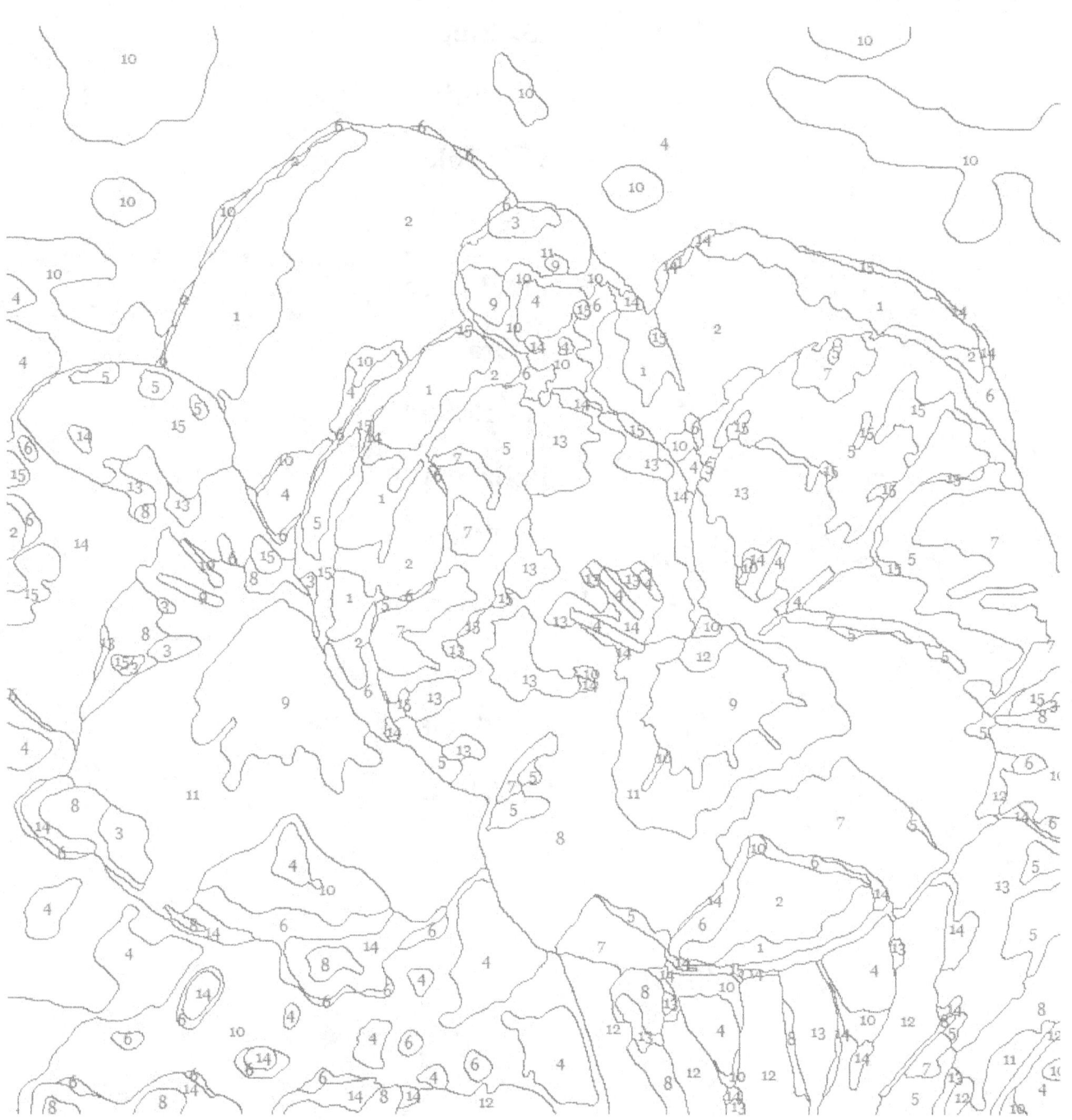

1. Red

2. Green

3. Blue

4. Pink

5. Purple

6. Light Blue

7. Light Green

8. Orange

9. Dark Red

10. Brown

11. Black

12. Dark Green

13. Gold

14. Violet

15. Yellow

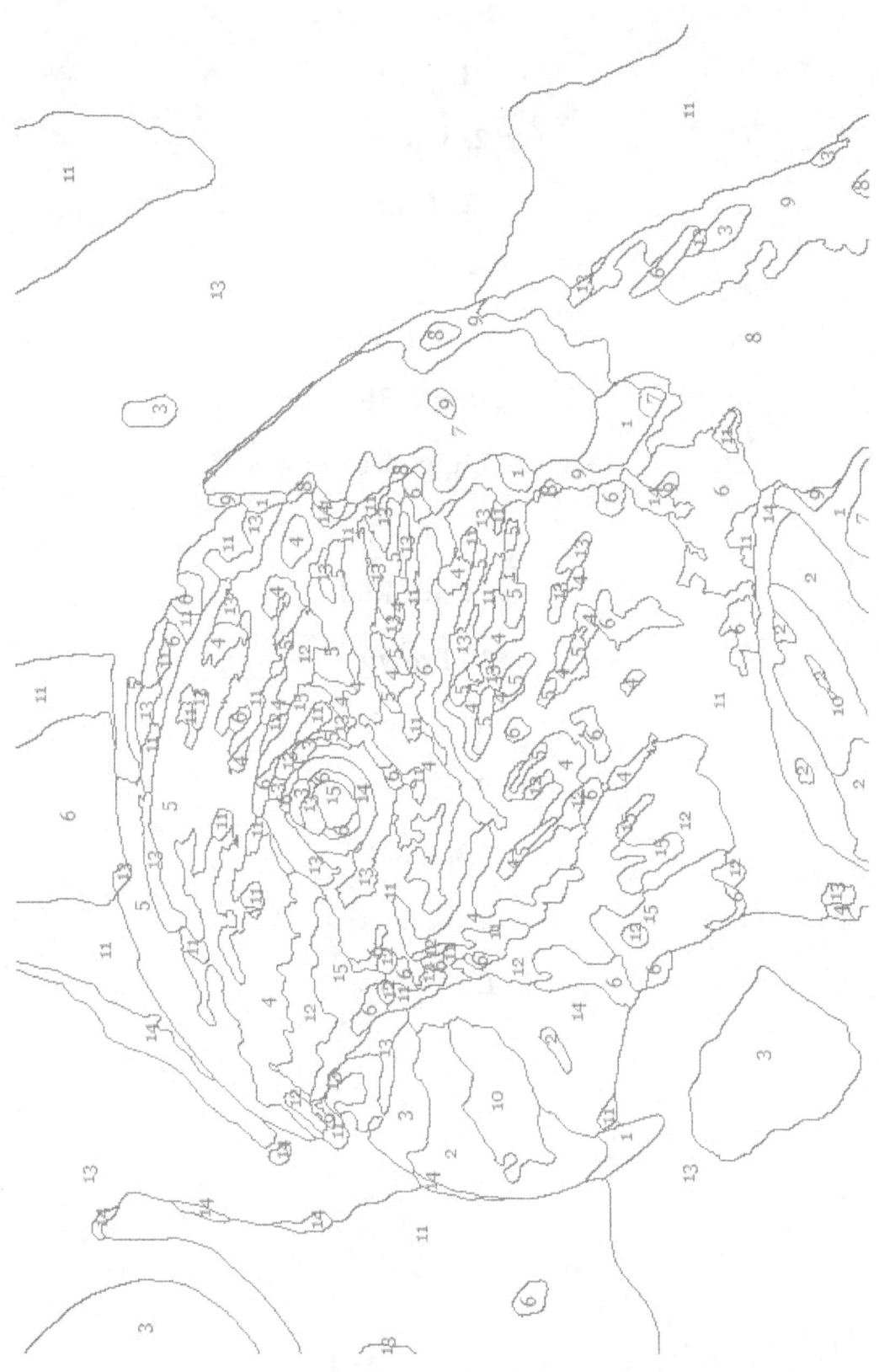

1. Red

2. Green

3. Blue

4. Pink

5. Purple

6. Light Blue

7. Light Green

8. Orange

9. Dark Red

10. Brown

11. Black

12. Dark Green

13. Gold

14. Violet

15. Yellow